16—43

1. *Literature for Individual Education*

> Esther Raushenbush. New York: Columbia University Press, 1942.

2. *Psychology for Individual Education*

> Lois B. Murphy, Eugene Lerner, Jane Judge, Madeleine Grant. Edited by Esther Raushenbush. New York: Columbia University Press, 1942.

3. *Teaching the Individual*

> Ruth Munroe. New York: Columbia University Press, 1942.

4. *Emotional Factors in Learning*

> Lois B. Murphy and Henry Ladd. New York: Columbia University Press, 1944.

5. *Field Work in College Education*

> Helen Merrell Lynd. New York: Columbia University Press, 1945.

6. *A Graduate Program in an Undergraduate College: The Sarah Lawrence Experience*

> Members of the Committee on Graduate Studies. Edited by Charles Trinkaus. Middletown (Conn.): Wesleyan University Press, 1956.

A Graduate Program

in an Undergraduate College

SARAH LAWRENCE COLLEGE PUBLICATIONS NO. 6

A Graduate Program
in an Undergraduate College

THE SARAH LAWRENCE EXPERIENCE

by members of the
COMMITTEE ON GRADUATE STUDIES
Sarah Lawrence College

EDITED BY CHARLES TRINKAUS

Wesleyan University Press

MIDDLETOWN, CONNECTICUT : 1956

Library of Congress Catalog Card Number: 56-12595

Contents

APPENDIXES

Introduction

THERE IS common agreement that things are not going as well as they might in the graduate schools. The troubles fall into two parts: too few first-rate students are applying; the graduate programs now in existence are producing trained specialists but too few imaginative scholars and teachers.

Educators in the field of science are deeply concerned about the decline in the number of science students now in graduate school (30,000 fewer graduates in 1954 than in 1950), about the unhappy situation in high school science teaching, about the narrow specialism of the majority of science graduates, and about the trend away from pure science into applied research and engineering. Some educators who are concerned about the place of the arts in American culture deplore the lack of interest in the study of the humanities in the undergraduate and graduate curriculum. Others are heavily critical of the academic courses in the humanities as they are now taught in the colleges. Many others are concerned about the quality and number of students in graduate schools of education, and about the quality of the work they do there. The law schools, the medical schools, and the business schools are the only graduate institutions which seem to be receiving the students they wish in sufficient numbers, although even here we find demands for students whose undergraduate education has been less specialized and more liberal than those now entering graduate work.

According to a report of the National Science Foundation on 152,067 resident students in graduate schools in 1954, 34 per cent were enrolled in education, 20 per cent in the natural sciences, 10 per cent in the social sciences, and 6 per cent in the humanities and the arts. It is clear from these statistics that there is very good reason to be concerned about the place of the liberal arts in the colleges and in the life of the country.

Presumably the colleges and universities can and will do something more about the revision of graduate school curricula to counteract the severity of the present specialized training and to develop better educated graduates. These reforms have been talked about during the whole of this century, by everyone from William James to Alfred North Whitehead. We cannot afford to allow the doctoral programs to continue in their present form. In this form they do not develop the kind of teachers the country needs.

However, as far as the shortage of graduate students is concerned, this is due to causes beyond the power of the universities to cure. The low birth rate of the depression years has meant a temporarily smaller population of college students on which to draw. With the lack of a substitute for the veterans' program, which amounted to a national subsidy for most of the country's young men who wished to go to college, there has been a decline in the total financial support given to undergraduate and graduate students. College students can find such a variety of attractive careers which will bring financial and social independence fairly quickly that they are unwilling to spend their own or their parents' money and three to five years of their time after college to take graduate training to enter a career in an ill-paid profession.

Whatever the causes, and there are many others, this is a very bad time for the shortage of graduate students to show itself. Beneath all the concern for the situation in the graduate schools lies the gnawing fact that even at present we do not have enough good teachers for the colleges and universities, and that with the present number of students now beginning graduate work, we will not have enough teachers, scholars, and research workers, either for the colleges or the high schools, to deal with the radical increase in the number of students who we know will be there during the next five to ten years. The difficulties are compounded when we realize that even if a national program of financial support and recruitment of graduate students were put into effect right away, there are at present not enough first-rate teachers who have resisted the lures of research grants, projects, consultation posts, government service, and industrial positions to teach them.

These are discouraging facts. But there are some encouraging ones connected with them. Recent studies by the Commission on Human Resources and Advanced Training show that we have a wealth of potential talent waiting to be educated if we can find the means of arranging it. About 152,000 of the 2,200,000 persons reaching the age of 18 each year achieve a score on intelligence tests which indicates an ability substantially higher than that of the average college graduate. "Although nearly all of this especially talented group finishes high school, only slightly over half enters college. Fewer than half finish college, and under 2 per cent receive Ph.D. degrees."[1] The Commission points out that "giving a college education to only half of the potentially most promising 7 per cent of the nation's youth constitutes a gross under-utilization of some of its highest talent."[2]

There are many reasons why only half of this potentially talented group of young people do not go to college, and many other reasons why so few of those who do go stop short of graduation or of going on to graduate school. The colleges should be able to do something about the half who do not finish after starting, either by improved selection or by an improved curriculum, but there are only two main things they can do about increasing the numbers of graduate students.

The first is to make of the undergraduate and graduate program such a combination of significant intellectual and personal experiences that the student will come to recognize in the work of the college teacher that high calling which has always marked the profession of the true scholar and the true teacher. Too often the experience of the student is one which makes him consider the undergraduate years as a time spent in meeting academic requirements for a degree which will help him to find an executive position in business and industry. As a result, the love of learning and the love of teaching seldom have a chance to develop. The crucial point in the encouragement of students to become teachers and scholars is in the attitude of college teachers toward their own work and toward their students during the undergraduate years.

The second is to do everything possible to draw public attention to the need for a radical increase in public support for the colleges and universities, through gifts to scholarship and fellowship funds,

[1] Waterman, Alan T., "The Science of Producing Good Scientists," in the magazine section of *The New York Times,* July 31, 1955.

[2] Quoted by Waterman, *loc. cit.*

to faculty salary budgets, through state and federal scholarship and loan programs, through unrestricted gifts from industry for the liberal arts and sciences, through foundation grants to develop programs of undergraduate and graduate study. Fortunately, there is already an awareness in the general public of the extent of these educational and cultural needs, and the Fund for the Advancement of Education, the Ford Foundation, the Carnegie Corporation, the Rockefeller Foundation, the National Merit Scholarship Fund, as well as an increasing number of business corporations, are spending their money directly on these needs. However, the colleges and the universities have not yet begun to receive the funds they must have if they are to solve the problems which the country has placed in their hands. We must have a very broad base of well-educated high school and college students from every segment of the country's population—Negro and white, poor and rich, workers and managers, urban and rural, North, South, East, and West, professional and business. From all those who can rise to higher levels of intellectual achievement, we must then choose those with the most talent for higher studies and support them to the hilt with money and encouragement. We must provide for them an intellectual environment which is exciting and provocative. It will take more than a billion dollars to make the right beginning. The country has the money, and ways must be found to direct it where it is most needed.

IN THE MEANTIME, the smaller residential colleges for the liberal arts have special opportunities and obligations for developing good graduate students. These colleges are certainly unable to help in a massive way to produce the number of scholars and teachers needed for the future, but they have the best opportunity of all to concentrate on new ways of lending the personal resources of their campus communities to the development of thoroughly trained, interested and interesting young teachers. In saying this, I do not mean that the college of liberal arts should turn its energies away from its central mission in the spread and increase of humane learning. I mean that the student who is committed to an honest effort to enrich and deepen his perceptions and his knowledge is at the same time one who is on the way to spreading that knowledge and using his perception in the society in which he lives. He is on his way to becoming a teacher. There is no essential difference between the student who loves learning and the student who is being prepared to teach what he knows to others. The true student will unavoidably teach what he knows, directly and indirectly, because he cannot help being interested in talking with other people about the matters which interest him.

Studies of the origins of the scholars and scientists of this country show that the largest proportion of them took their undergraduate degrees in the smaller residential liberal arts colleges, moving to graduate work in professional schools and universities when advanced instruction was not available in the smaller institutions. The high proportion is natural, since the chances are greater that in the community life of a small residential college, the student will gain a deeper sense of the purpose and significance of his education through a closer association with his teachers and contemporaries than is possible in the larger universities. Too often we forget that the best reason for the student to go to graduate school is that he wants to know more about something of which he has learned a little, and that a fascination with the ideas and problems of a given area of knowledge drives him on to further inquiry. We have not paid enough attention to the emotional and personal factors in the impulse of the young student toward further study. The crucial period in the development of a first-rate graduate student is in the development of the student as an undergraduate. Where else, except perhaps from the influence of a parent, a relative or friend, will the student receive the impulse to continue his learning in advanced studies? Once the talented student has been seized by an interest in the higher learning, he can work his own way through almost any program of graduate studies, whether it be well or badly organized, secure in his own conviction that the program will yield him the knowledge he seeks and that it is there to be found. But he must *want* to know before he will engage himself fully in the whole enterprise.

If the undergraduate is to move into the graduate field, there should be a close relation between the undergraduate and the graduate curriculum in a given institution. This may not be possible in the large university, where the graduate schools are separate entities and little effort is made to develop them as a phase of higher education which builds upon and goes beyond the undergraduate content and method. A great deal of the time the matter is put the other way around. Much of the undergraduate curriculum is composed of courses which are useful principally for meeting the requirements of admission to graduate schools, as if the assumption were made that all undergraduates went to and will go to graduate school. This is a great deterrent to the development of serious interest by the student in the undergraduate curriculum, since it reduces a great deal of the undergraduate course content to a series of technical studies. This also accounts for much of the artificial separation of subject matter into departments, and puts an over-emphasis on "covering" subjects. Pre-medical, pre-law, pre-dental, pre-education, and other pre- curricula are made, and the pattern of courses is set, not by the generous idea that through it the student may come to love learning and to understand its place in his life, but by the earth-bound notion that it will help him to get into the graduate school of his choice.

But in the smaller institutions, the pressures toward patterning are, or at least should be, less. The methods of the graduate school at its best, that is to say, independent research projects, seminars, tutorial instruction, some freedom of choice among fields and subjects, consideration of the student as an adult, can become part of the undergraduate program. In some of the smaller colleges, as well as in a few of the larger Eastern colleges, independent work can be carried on by juniors or seniors in a style not very different from the advanced graduate student. At Sarah Lawrence our experience has shown that a great deal of this kind of independence and responsibility can and should be given to freshmen, and that it is not necessary, or desirable, to circumscribe the undergraduate student with academic rules and requirements, thus reducing the area of his own responsibility. If he is given this responsibility on entering college, he is likely to accept it, to thrive with it, and to think of graduate school, when he does so, with a sense of anticipation of further learning.

There are other connections between the undergraduate and the graduate program. The first year of graduate study is a special year in the life of the graduate. Although it has a quality different from the freshman year in college, the first year of graduate school contains some of the same problems. As in the case of the freshman year, an unsuccessful first year in graduate school is most often the result of a failure to find a sense of purpose in academic study or it is due to a lack of serious intellectual purpose in being in graduate school at all. Once a student is in an undergraduate college, it is possible for him to go on from year to year from a sense of general obligation rather than from a desire to pursue a known goal. Many college students, I think most college students, do not come to college with a specific goal toward which they believe their studies will take them. They are more likely to assume that they will find these goals in college, or that, by continuing there, they will fulfill the expectations of their families. Or they assume that taking the degree is an end in itself.

Many of those who enter graduate school are in the same state of mind—they assume that by following the curriculum as indicated they will prepare themselves for a post of some kind, but they are unclear as to the purpose which a given study will serve in relation to their own personal values and interests and in relation to their total development as scholars or teachers. On the other hand, the graduate schools are organized on the assumption that those who come know why they are there and what to do about it. This is as it should be if we are dealing with entering students who have thought carefully about what their education has meant and why they wish to continue it. But it may result in the loss of some potentially able graduate students who simply need to learn, when they have not already done so, the use to which their knowledge can be put, and the relation which graduate work has to their ultimate purposes. Educators in the graduate schools must be conscious of the fact that they are dealing with students who begin with a first year, and that the first year is the crucial one in determining whether or not the student will eventually become a teacher and a scholar. It is also a crucial period in determining what kind of teacher and scholar the student will become. There are many graduate students who are drawn toward higher studies by a general interest in ideas and for whom the single most important need in the first year of graduate work is for wise and friendly help by teachers in deciding what particular studies to undertake. This is not a matter of placement tests or measured aptitudes but a matter of the student examining interesting alternatives in the company of an older person who knows a good deal about what these alternatives involve.

In the sample taken by the National Science Foundation, in 1954, 96,000 students were in their first year, 58,000 had gone further. Of the 96,000 first-year students, many will have given up graduate study by 1955, some because of lack of motivation to continue, some because of the attraction of other pursuits. But many of these students attended graduate school with the intention of remaining for only one year to take a degree of Master of Arts, or Master of Science, particularly in the field of education or in a subject-matter field which the individual is teaching in the high school curriculum. As Helen McMaster has pointed out in the opening pages of Chapter One of this book, the content of the M.A. degree is extremely mixed and varies widely from college to college, although the purpose in taking it is most often for adding a higher degree to the Bachelor of Arts with the consequent increase in the range of possibility for academic or other employment. Many teachers spend their evenings and their summers in taking courses which will gradually yield the correct number of credits for the higher degree. I do not mean to make an invidious comparison between those who are motivated by academic ambition and those who are "true" scholars. But I think it important to recognize that the essential purpose of the Master of Arts degree has been obscured by the relation it bears to academic advancement. As President Barnaby Keeney of Brown University is quoted as saying later in this book, the Master of Arts degree needs to be rehabilitated, and its character re-established as a special degree which is not merely a credit-gathering enterprise or a first step toward a doctorate. It may be the latter, and we may be grateful that it is. However, the degree of Master of Arts must have an integrity of its own and it only does so when it helps the student to establish a solid basis of knowledge and purpose with which to continue his education and his interest in ideas.

Those of us who have responsibility in the appointment of faculty members to college posts are sometimes bewildered by the fact that the process of taking the doctorate has so often resulted in the destruction of the spontaneous and lively interest of the candidate in the field of teaching and scholarship itself. Our policy in the appointment of faculty members at Sarah Lawrence College has been not to place degree requirements in a central position among our expectations, but to consider the quality of the candidate's total experience, the extent of his knowledge, and the possibilities he shows for creative work in teaching. We assume that a person who is seriously interested in teaching will, of course, be interested in scholarship, that he will read deeply and widely in the field of his interest, but we do not assume that every person who does so will publish monographs, books, and pamphlets, or that every scholar should have a higher degree. Publication is a matter of the personal aptitude and interest of the teacher. He may prefer to bring the fruits of his scholarship only to his students, and he may find his best means of expression of that scholarship in the daily opportunity of working with students in class discussion and conference. On the other hand, the person who works with students may find that, through the process of bringing to them the available scholarship in his field, he has developed something which he would like to say to a wider audience. He may then begin to write and to publish. But the central point in his development as a teacher remains the transmission of what he knows to his students and the re-creation by them of the knowledge which they are trying to make their own. In this way the scholar-teacher has a continuous stream of comment from friendly critics and a rich source of new suggestion and fresh insight which can stimulate his own imagination as a scholar.

It is not altogether clear, therefore, that the most appropriate preparation for college teaching in the arts and the humanities is to take the degree of Doctor of Philosophy. What matters most is that the student learn a great deal, by whatever formal or informal means, about the field of knowledge to which he is drawn by natural interests, and that he learn to teach by associating closely with good teachers in a college environment. I believe that this can best be done in graduate studies which are closely related to an undergraduate program. Some of the most interesting experiments with this approach have been made possible by the Fund for the Advancement of Education and the Carnegie Corporation, and it is to be expected that the liberal arts colleges may, within the limits of their financial resources, continue this way of encouraging graduate students to prepare for a teaching career. It is certainly true that this is one of the most useful ways in which the first year of graduate study, leading toward the degree of Master of Arts, can be spent. It has the effect of making clear the purpose of graduate study while the study itself is being conducted. It may also have the effect of preparing the graduate student thoroughly for the continuation of graduate study toward the doctorate, if the higher degree, as in the case of the natural sciences, is a necessary step toward the mastery of a given body of knowledge. The role of the smaller residential colleges in work of this kind is obviously an important one, and although it may not be possible for such colleges to offer the doctorate in every field, it is usually possible to offer the Master of Arts degree in each of the major areas of study. At Sarah Lawrence we found, during a conference on this and related topics, that there was common agreement to this point of view on the part of a sampling of the smaller liberal arts colleges in the East in which the Master of Arts degree is offered.[3]

WITH MANY of these ideas in mind, and with a feeling of responsibility toward the need for new teachers, the faculty of Sarah Lawrence College and its administrative officers began seven years ago to make plans for an experiment in graduate studies. We discovered very quickly that this was a project of large proportion, since it involved the time and energy of faculty members who were already fully occupied with the undergraduate program, and it demanded the re-examination and rethinking of the whole process of selection of students, the graduate curriculum, finance, housing, the advisory system, and the relation of the new program to the undergraduate curriculum.

The undergraduate program at Sarah Lawrence was established in 1928, when the College opened, as an experiment in the reform of liberal education. In place of the conventional curriculum of the elective system or of the required sequences of departmental courses, the faculty has built a program in which each student plans an individual curriculum of courses with the help of faculty advisers. In addition to the general curriculum of liberal arts, the creative arts, painting, drawing, sculpture, music, design, theatre, dance, and writing have been installed as regular elements of the curriculum itself. Instruction is conducted by the seminar and discussion method, with regular weekly conferences between the faculty member and his students, and the lecture used only occasionally when it is considered appropriate. Science is taught in the laboratory with student research; theatre is taught on the stage as well as in the classroom; social science through field projects; child psychology in the nursery school; literature, history, philosophy through original sources with only occasional reference to textbooks, anthologies, or surveys. The aim throughout the teaching program is to confront the student directly with the materials and methods of each branch of knowledge and to make them real in

[3] See Chapter Four, "Master of Arts Programs in Small Colleges: The Need for a New Concept," by Joseph Campbell.

his experience. Courses are planned on a full-year basis, and, in a given year, students work in three courses rather than the usual five or six. There are no organized departments, and no majors, although students who wish to work in a given field as one-third of the year's program throughout the whole four years are usually allowed to do so. Field work is a regular part of each section of the curriculum. The examination, grading, and credit system is replaced by a system of reports made three times each year by the faculty members on the basis of the work of the student in class, in independent research projects, and in conference. There are no subject-matter requirements for graduation other than the successful completion of four years of study as approved by a faculty committee which supervises the course of study of each student. The student body and the faculty were granted self-governing powers by the original Board of Trustees and administer their affairs by elected committees. There are no faculty ranks.

The character of the undergraduate program has remained unchanged in these essentials over the years since the College began, although variations in method and approach have been introduced as research has shown places where reforms were needed. The freshman year, for example, has evolved to a design in which the student is initially assigned to a course known as exploratory, with the teacher of the course assigned to act as adviser to the beginning student. The exploratory course has no syllabus or subject matter set in advance, but develops its own subject matter, reading assignments, and projects as the students and the teacher work together. These courses are taught by the most experienced members of the Sarah Lawrence faculty in the fields of literature, psychology, social science, and the visual arts. They are an attempt to help the student to learn how various forms of knowledge are interrelated, how to explore a variety of subjects and topics, and how to proceed with her own education. In addition to the work of the exploratory course, the freshman works in two other fields during the year.

With this background in experimental philosophy and the experience of developing a new undergraduate program in the liberal arts, it was natural for the Sarah Lawrence faculty to wish to apply what had been learned to the problem of graduate education. This book is a study of the problems involved in trying to realize the philosophy of individual education in a program of graduate work. It is based on the first four years of trial and error in such a program at Sarah Lawrence, and is written in the hope that our experience may be useful to other colleges and to others interested in the field of graduate education. We would not have been able to begin without the help of the Carnegie Corporation, whose then-president, Charles Dollard, and his colleague, Oliver Carmichael, studied our proposals, came to the campus, talked with us about our work and our plans and, in co-operation with the Carnegie Board of Trustees, made arrangements for a grant of $50,000 to be given to the College to begin our work. Any person who has wrestled with the problem of adding a new program of graduate studies to an undergraduate college which has already spent all its money and most of its time on the undergraduates will understand the importance to us of the Carnegie grant, and the extent of our gratitude to the Corporation for its help in making our experiment possible.

The book owes its existence to the work of Dean Esther Raushenbush, who has been a central figure in planning and carrying out the program; to Mrs. Helen McMaster who served for four years on the Committee on Graduate Studies and acted as its chairman in 1953-54; to Mrs. Jane Judge and Mr. Joseph Campbell, members of the Committee; and to Mr. Charles Trinkaus, present chairman of the Committee on Graduate Studies, who has served as editor. The College is very grateful to them for their part in building the graduate program and in making this account of it available to other educators.

HAROLD TAYLOR

Bronxville, New York
June, 1956

A Graduate Program

in an Undergraduate College

CHAPTER ONE

Getting the Program Started

HELEN McMASTER

THE DEGREE of Master of Arts is especially ill-defined in American education, although thousands of such degrees are awarded every year, and the label is increasingly required for the pursuit of any teaching career from the nursery school on. The liberal arts college in the United States as distinct from the university or professional school has engaged primarily in the education of young men and women who wish to qualify for the A.B. degree. The various states in granting charters to colleges set down certain principles which aim at insuring some uniformity in the attainments symbolized by the degree. In addition, accrediting associations in each geographical area have been established to review the work of the colleges at appropriate intervals, and to give recognition to the maintenance of proper standards through published reports. Although the individual colleges represent a wide variety of educational ideas and standards and the recipients of an A.B. are not a group uniformly trained, at least there is a general understanding of the significance of the educational experience of the recipient of the A.B. Moreover, the standards and requirements demanded for the degree of Doctor of Philosophy vary from one university to another, but the differences are in degree or quality, not in kind. Every Ph.D. program requires a specialized knowledge of a subject, and professes to require evidence that the candidate can do original research, and that he demonstrate this ability by writing a dissertation embodying such research.

An examination of the Master's program in some of our best colleges and universities indicates how diversely it has been conceived. This degree may be a mild imitation of a Doctor's degree, or it may be an extension of the education undertaken in qualifying for an A.B., the passing of graduate courses with a "B" average; or it may

3

be neither of these. The difficulty lies not so much in the fact that the meaning of the degree differs from one institution to another, as the fact that the intention in any given instance is often unclear. From descriptive statements in catalogues, a student with a clear-cut purpose in qualifying for an M.A. would have difficulty in making a proper choice.

Very little serious and concerted thought seems to have been given to the purposes to be served by the M.A. In one institution the M.A. may be regarded as a useful test in selecting candidates for the Ph.D. In another, the M.A. is offered as a way of attracting graduate students who can act as assistants in various departments. In most institutions the character of the M.A. has evolved in a haphazard rather than a planned way. The reasons for acquiring an A.B. or a Ph.D. are better understood by the candidates for such degrees than the reasons for acquiring the M.A., and the values are more fully recognized by those employing the successful candidates. Yet the M.A. is being required of applicants for a variety of positions in teaching and in other fields. Why is this requirement made? Do those employing qualified M.A. graduates have some particular expectation in mind? Answers to these questions are not readily available.

There is little to be gained by trying to give any single definition of the M.A., or to settle upon any single plan of requirements. A year of graduate work may well serve a variety of purposes. One of the traditional functions of the M.A. has been the furthering of the qualifications of teachers for their profession. For this purpose, one might expect some uniformity of opinion among educators about the kind of work the degree should represent.

The importance of the liberal arts college for the preparation of teachers

WHEN IT became evident that the annual recipients of the A.B. who went into teaching were insufficient in numbers to provide the teachers needed for our growing school population, various new types of training schools for teachers were founded by states and supported by tax money. Universities, privately supported, concerned themselves with special programs for teachers. Both public and private institutions have exerted themselves in trying to meet the needs.

4

Unfortunately, in the process of trying to produce a sufficient number of well-trained teachers as rapidly as possible, and at a reasonable cost in time and money to the potential teacher, what now seems a false division of opinion of how this could be done arose among educators. Those who wished to use a maximum amount of the student's time for training in methods of teaching hoped that further knowledge in subject matter would be acquired in the process of teaching. Those who wished to use a maximum amount of the student's time for the study of subject matter hoped that young people who wanted to teach would be "natural-born" teachers or would learn how in the process. The heated discussions within colleges, universities, and at meetings of educational associations were stimulated by fears on all sides that more and more children were suffering from incompetent teaching. In recent years many educators have come to realize that the problem will not be solved by a theoretical victory of either side. Discussions are now turning to what can be done about certain actualities that must be faced: a decreasing number of young people are attracted to teaching at any level; educational plans, whatever the degree of emphasis on subject matter or methods, have not produced enough teachers of the quality desired.

The existing economic and social factors which seem to make the profession of teaching unattractive to young people have become of general concern to parents and public-minded citizens as well as to teachers in the profession. While welcoming the aid of the laymen, the teaching profession must continue to work at its side of the problem. One step might be in re-directing the Master's degree toward the training of teachers. This would mean an examination of methods and procedures in institutions now offering the degree. The recent innovations at several universities of a Master of Arts in Teaching indicates that some steps have already been taken. This is not necessarily the only way of meeting the present situation. Within the framework of individual institutions with an established Master of Arts program, other solutions may be more appropriate. Liberal arts colleges which have not heretofore offered work for the M.A. might well consider what they could contribute toward the education of potential teachers. Such colleges have an advantage in that they can begin planning in terms of present thinking unencumbered by previous commitments to plans which have not proved to be ideal solutions.

*How the idea of a graduate studies program
originated at Sarah Lawrence College*

A LIBERAL ARTS COLLEGE which contemplates adding work at the graduate level leading to the M.A. degree needs to consider very carefully why this work is being contemplated, how it is to be carried out, and the implications for both the faculty and the undergraduates. Although liberal arts colleges in general are united by a common objective, each liberal arts college has developed in its individual way. As a consequence there is no single ideal way of introducing and administering a program of graduate studies. The plan must grow out of and become a part of the life of the college in question.

Studies of existing graduate programs in colleges of comparable size are useful; conversations with members of the faculties of such institutions are helpful. Much can be learned from the experience of others, but in the end the best way to insure a successful program is to begin with a careful review of the current situation at the home college and an analysis of *why* graduate work is being considered. The way in which a particular college has come to the consideration is one of the factors influencing the development of the program.

At Sarah Lawrence College, certain members of the faculty came to be interested in graduate work in one of several ways. In 1947, at the suggestion of the Department of Higher Education of New York University's School of Education, a Summer Workshop for teachers who were candidates for graduate degrees at New York University was organized at Sarah Lawrence College. Seminars, planned according to the special educational procedures followed at Sarah Lawrence College, were conducted by appropriate members of the Sarah Lawrence faculty. The candidates attending these summer workshops in the summers of 1947 and 1948 were men and women with experience in college or secondary school teaching. Their response to the brief educational experience of Sarah Lawrence teaching methods on a graduate level was enthusiastic. The Sarah Lawrence faculty who worked with them felt that the College could offer to teachers many values which are not available at larger universities.

In another part of the College, Sarah Lawrence teachers be-

6

came interested in offering the M.A. degree. Since the foundation of the College, extensive work in early childhood education has been offered to undergraduates. The Sarah Lawrence College Nursery School, established in 1935, has gained national recognition, and graduates, qualified in this field, have been in demand as teachers in private nursery schools. With the need for more teachers in early childhood education in public schools, the Sarah Lawrence College faculty concerned took up the matter of preparing graduates for certification to teach kindergarten and early grades in public schools. Plans were worked out so that a student who knew early enough in her college career that she wished to teach children, could meet the requirements for certification in New York State while she was qualifying for the A.B. degree. In this field of teaching, as in others, advancement often depends on qualifying for the M.A. The Bank Street College of Education, a professional school eminent in the field of nursery school education, made inquiries about the possibility of a joint plan by which their students could qualify for the M.A. at Sarah Lawrence College.

Members of the faculty not directly connected either with the summer workshops or the nursery school were frequently asked by former students or friends of former students about the possibility of graduate work at Sarah Lawrence College. There seemed to be comparatively few colleges and universities at which students in the arts could qualify for an M.A. with a major part of their time devoted to composing music, to painting, to sculpture, to choreography and participation in dance, to active work in the theatre. Students in science, social studies, and literature were also looking for a college in which it was possible to combine literature and history or to make other appropriate combinations which are not possible in highly-departmentalized graduate work.

The possibility of undertaking some graduate work became a topic of conversation among the faculty as a whole. The question whether Sarah Lawrence College would attempt to add work for the M.A. was referred for consideration to the Planning Committee in the fall of 1948. After several discussions and meetings with representatives of the various groups, the Planning Committee recommended "if possible and as soon as possible" that graduate work be added to the work of the College. The recommendation was discussed in a meeting of the faculty on March 1, 1949. Opinions as to the desirability of this addition varied widely; however, at the end of the meeting the faculty voted "to ask the President to apply to the Board of Regents for the privilege of granting an M.A. degree and to empower the Planning Committee to study the problems and procedures in connection with graduate study at Sarah Lawrence College." The Planning Committee appointed a sub-committee to work with President Taylor and Dean Raushenbush.

Mr. Taylor and the Sarah Lawrence Board of Trustees took up the matter with the Board of Regents of the University of the State of New York, which formally voted on July 15, 1949, to amend the charter of Sarah Lawrence College authorizing the College to grant the degree of Master of Arts.

In the process of obtaining this authorization, a good deal of excellent advice from members of the Education Department of the State of New York, from members of the Sarah Lawrence Trustee Committee on Education, and from faculties engaged in graduate work at other institutions had been gathered and considered. As yet little thought had been given to ways and means of carrying out a program in which Sarah Lawrence methods of undergraduate education would be applied in the field of graduate study.[1]

Preliminary planning and initial decisions concerning administrative procedures, finances, general purposes, admissions requirements, and public announcement

DECISIONS needed to be made about the cost of tuition, the number of graduate students to be admitted each year, the requirements for admission, the provision of faculty time for teaching graduate students on an individual basis, and the requirements for the degree. At Sarah Lawrence College, under a grant of powers made by the Board of Trustees, the teaching staff and the college administration constitute the faculty which participates as a body through central committees in planning curriculum and in evaluating work. Such group or departmental organization as exists is purely informal, at liberty to recommend ideas to the central committees, but final decisions on educational policy and administration remain with the elected faculty committees. This situation saved the College from some of the pitfalls about which it had been warned in

[1] See Appendix I.

colleges where decisions about graduate work rested with heads of departments and the Dean. The natural way of handling graduate work at Sarah Lawrence College was inevitably through a central committee. Since the authorization to grant the M.A. occurred during the summer holiday, an initial committee of three members was appointed by the President to be known as the Committee on Graduate Studies. In the fall the Committee became a regularly elected committee of the faculty with one new member to be elected annually for a three-year term.

This Committee found that certain of the questions were answered for them by the existing pattern of education in the United States. Tuitions charged candidates for advanced degrees throughout the country were low and fairly uniform, averaging about $500 a year. Families who have carried the cost of undergraduate education are frequently not able to help graduate students, who for the most part are of an age when their earning capacity is minimal. The cost of educating a graduate student is far in excess of any practical fee. The answer to availability of faculty time for graduate students could only be met by an addition to the faculty in proportion to the number of graduate students admitted. Funds commensurate with the need must be found to add to the faculty salary budget. To interest donors, plans must be made and possibly put into operation. The Committee postponed further talk about finances and went on to consider educational plans for graduate work.[2]

As soon as the Committee could formulate some general principles, such conclusions as they had arrived at were presented to the faculty. The faculty accepted with little discussion the statement of basic policy:

> The basic purpose and objectives of graduate instruction at Sarah Lawrence College are to be the same as the principles which operate in the College. As in the College, no formal over-all program is to be designed. Advanced study is to be planned in terms of individual student needs and individual student purposes, not in terms of credits and courses.

The Committee statement relative to the framework within which this policy was to be carried out aroused active discussion:

[2] See Appendix II for a statement on financing the Sarah Lawrence program.

9

While no student will be recommended for the degree after less than a full year of academic work, a year of work will not necessarily earn the degree. Rather, competence and maturity, and demonstrated ability to fulfill the program originally set forth, are suggested as the criteria. These are to be judged by the faculty concerned with such help as the Committee on Graduate Studies can give. Together, they will determine whether the degree will be awarded. Therefore, students will be admitted only after they have satisfied the faculty with whom they are to work that they are best fitted for the kind of study offered here. The acquisition of a degree by the accumulation of part-time work over a long span of time is to be discouraged.

The faculty quite naturally wanted clarification about the way acceptance by the Committee and the particular teacher would work out. What would the requirements for entrance be? The Committee was clear about the first point: the decision about acceptance would be mutual. The Committee would not accept a student it thought generally qualified for graduate work if the teacher who would be principally involved in the teaching of the student did not consider the candidate qualified. Conversely, no members of the faculty could accept a graduate student who had not been rated as generally acceptable by the Committee. The reasons for an individual teacher refusing to accept a particular candidate, whatever these reasons might be, would be respected by the Committee. In a graduate program such as was contemplated, the mutual respect and compatibility of the teacher and the student are basic to any success in carrying out the objectives.

As to the requirements for entrance as a candidate, the Committee recommended, in addition to the usual requirements (evidence of academic competence at an accredited undergraduate institution, letters of recommendation, and an interview), that the admissions material include a questionnaire similar to the one used for undergraduates. The purpose of this questionnaire would be to bring out, if possible, the personal qualifications of the applicant for the goal or goals he had in mind in undertaking graduate study. The Committee asked the faculty to consider the types of student each would think desirable, the kinds of background, and variety of training essential for advanced work in a chosen field. Members of the faculty, either as individuals or in groups, were asked to submit their ideas either orally or in writing to the Committee.

The relation of the Committee on Graduate Studies to the committee structure of the College was a matter of concern to many members of the faculty. Quite a number were in favor of having its functions absorbed by the regular committee structure: the Admissions Committee to consider graduate applicants along with undergraduate; the Committee on Student Work to decide about awarding the M.A. as well as the A.B. degree. This group of the faculty obviously wanted to avoid an autonomous Graduate School, or even a graduate program that might overshadow the undergraduate work. The absorption by these committees of the work of the Committee on Graduate Studies has not occurred, but chiefly for practical reasons involving the amount and timing of work involved which could not be added to the duties of the established undergraduate committees.

The discussion was carried over and continued in a second faculty meeting. At the end of this meeting a motion was passed which authorized the appointed Committee to continue to function in initiating the program. There was general agreement that a tuition fee of $500 would be appropriate, that not more than ten students be accepted in a single year, and for the first year possibly only two or three students. The Committee on Graduate Studies was asked to prepare an announcement for the public about the nature of the program and to work out a suitable questionnaire; both of these to be submitted to the faculty for final approval.

The Committee on Graduate Studies began an attempt to formulate a descriptive statement about the graduate program. No three members of any faculty, even after general faculty discussions, can sit down and write such a statement without further exploration of faculty sentiment. A number of the faculty had responded to the request to submit their ideas in writing. The Committee decided to have conversations with each member of the faculty in which he would be asked questions about his interest in graduate work, requirements for graduate work in his subject, and his ideas about suitable programs. Any teacher who believed that graduate work in his subject should not be undertaken could be reassured that this would not be done. Others who felt that their fields offered special opportunities could outline specific requirements for candidates and suggest the kinds of programs which they thought could be effectively carried on. Such an informal procedure was practical at Sarah Lawrence College with a faculty of approximately seventy-five people. Each member of the Committee interviewed some twenty-five individuals. Although this meant some delay in preparing the statement about the graduate program, the time was well spent in terms of involving the whole faculty in the thinking that went into the incorporation of graduate work into the plans of Sarah Lawrence College. Reactions to the idea of a graduate program ranged from enthusiastic to tolerant; no group of the faculty was actively opposed to some graduate work being offered. It would seem that some such general acceptance of the addition of graduate work to the undergraduate curriculum is essential to the ultimate success of the program.

The Committee on Graduate Studies submitted a statement of the general plan of the program to the faculty late in November 1949. After some discussion the statement was approved. The President was urged to see what could be done about interesting possible donors. Sarah Lawrence College was most fortunate in gaining the generous support of the Carnegie Corporation for the venture for a period of four years.

Concurrent with interviewing the faculty and preparing the statement about the graduate program, the members of the Committee also worked on ways of determining the qualification of students. The A.B. from an accredited college was a first requirement; the selection of students to be made on (1) the undergraduate record, (2) a statement of purposes and goals of the candidate, (3) a personal interview, and (4) the completion of a written form. A transcript of the undergraduate record, along with letters from former teachers, is of value in direct proportion to what is known of the standards of the institution and of the individual teachers. Grades, be they numerical or alphabetical, are not absolutes. The Committee considered the use of the Graduate Record Examinations as a check on the undergraduate record in an effort to predict the possibility of a candidate's ability for academic success at the graduate level. The Educational Testing Service had just begun a two-year project of revising their tests in the light of their past experience. The Committee decided not to recommend, at least for the time being, the requirement of these tests. The Committee counted rather heavily on getting corroborative data from the

12

applicant's statement of his objectives in his initial letter inquiring about the program, from the interview, and from the answers to a series of questions—all of which would serve as a check on the undergraduate record.

At Sarah Lawrence College, admissions material for under-graduates has always included answers to two sets of questions: one to be answered by the prospective student and the other by the parents. The questions have no right or wrong answers; they are designed to call forth answers which give some insight into factors (not easily measured by grades) which affect the learning process. After several revisions of the original sets of questions, the replies of a given student and of her parents have proved to be most useful in estimating her motivation, drive, imagination, and general purpose, and the relation of these to the parents' aspirations.

For the graduate program, the Committee discovered that it would have to create a set of questions with very little to go on from the experience of others. In medicine, law, and engineering, aptitude tests have been used for some years in evaluating the fitness of the candidate for the practice of these professions. In relation to candidates for the M.A., the assumption seems to have been that anyone with a good undergraduate record and the desire to qualify for the M.A. should be allowed to undertake the work.

The majority of candidates for the M.A. in the United States plan on teaching. Tests are available on mental ability, cultural backgrounds, and subject matter, but none of the available tests are aimed specifically at determining the qualities which make for a good teacher. At a conference on the Preparation of College Teachers, held at Chicago in December, 1949, the need for formulating personal criteria in addition to a knowledge of subject matter was stressed by Dean Harry J. Carman of Columbia University and Professor Lloyd S. Woodburne of the University of Michigan. Dean Carman said:

> . . . our liberal arts colleges want teachers who are persons of attractive personality, insight, sensitiveness, and perspective— persons who have a happy disposition and a sense of humor and who have the urge to be guides, philosophers, and friends of students—persons whom students seek out and index in their mind as grand persons and wonderful teachers. We need teachers who have moral strength, a sense of beauty of spirit, the

13

seeing eye, the watchful soul, the inquiring mind. We want teachers who are free from conventional prejudices and fears, and who are articulate and skilled in conversation. Above all, we want them to have a quenchless desire to instruct and inspire youth and to derive great satisfaction from assisting students to see the relationship between learning and life.[3]

Professor Woodburne listed as a "minimum" the essential qualities of the successful teacher:

1. Emotional control and maturity
2. A "B" average intellectual ability
3. A deep interest in students and other people
4. A vital enthusiasm for the subjects taught
5. Imagination, inventiveness, and curiosity
6. A strong drive and persistence[4]

Practically all of these highly desirable qualities are very difficult to estimate by tests or even in an interview. They are traits that we all value and learn about gradually in the course of day-by-day contact with students and friends. What kind of questions would bring out answers that would reveal the presence or absence of these qualities?

Realizing the difficulty of the task, the Committee on Graduate Studies set about devising questions which they hoped would evoke answers throwing some light on the personal qualifications of candidates for advanced work and especially for teaching. Many of the questions submitted by the Committee for the approval of the faculty were vetoed on the grounds that they were too "personal," insulting to an adult, or unnecessary for determining the eligibility of the candidate. The questions which were used in the first version of our questionnaire did not bring out the kinds of things that the Committee wanted to get at. After two revisions, the questionnaire has gradually become more useful. Many members of the faculty have modified their idea that candidates for graduate degrees necessarily know what they want or have made the best choice for a future career, and now see the value of such a questionnaire. In its

[3] *American Council on Education Studies*, Series I, No. 42 (Washington, D. C., July, 1950), Vol. XIV, p. 18.

[4] *Ibid.* p. 62.

present form, in addition to the usual statistical queries about date and place of birth, present home address, schools attended, and marital status, the following questions, appropriately spaced on an eight-page form, are asked:

1. Why do you wish to undertake graduate study?
2. What would you like to undertake specifically in a graduate program?
3. Describe in detail any special project you have carried out in any field of study.
4. (*a*) Name one book that you have read recently and liked; tell why.
   (*b*) Name one book that you have read recently and disliked; tell why.
5. In what ways has your education so far been most satisfactory?
6. In what ways has your education so far been unsatisfactory?
7. How have you spent your summers?
8. What have you done since leaving college?
9. What do you hope to do after completing graduate work?

Questions 1, 2, 3, and 9 are allotted a full page; the others half a page each. On the cover, below the statistical queries, the following statement appears: "This questionnaire should not be considered an examination. Answers are not judged right or wrong, but are expected to vary as individuals vary. It is important that you read through this form before you begin to write."

Although this version of the admissions form works better than its predecessors, the Committee hopes that with the cumulative experience gained from reading completed applications, and from testing expectations based upon interpretation of the answers against performance of accepted candidates, that further revisions may make the questionnaire even more effective in evaluating the personal factors which inevitably affect the learning process.

A descriptive statement about the nature of graduate work to be offered at Sarah Lawrence was completed and approved by the faculty in March 1950. The Committee was authorized to have this printed in leaflet form, suitable for mailing to prospective candidates. The statement in its present slightly-revised form is as follows:

Sarah Lawrence College offers a program of graduate studies in the liberal arts leading to the degree of Master of Arts. The fields in which work is offered include the social sciences, theatre, dance, music, the visual arts, psychology, nursery school training, literature, and the natural sciences.

A Committee on Graduate Studies, consisting of three faculty members, and the Dean of the College, is the central planning body for the Graduate Studies Program. On the basis of admissions material and conferences with the student, each candidate is assigned to a member of the faculty who will be his major teacher for the whole year or for a designated period. One member of the Graduate Studies Committee takes responsibility for following the work of each student through the year. The major teacher and the student consult with this member of the Committee, and together they plan for supplementary work. These plans are subject to approval by the Graduate Studies Committee.

Each student works intensively with his major teacher and with two, or in some cases three, other faculty members. Part of his work is done in regular courses, part in individual conferences. Each student is asked to undertake a project of a kind most suited to his talents and purposes. The project may consist of research in the social or natural sciences, creative work or research in the arts and in literature, field work, apprentice teaching or a thesis written on the basis of special knowledge in a given field.

The faculty teaching a particular graduate student meet monthly to discuss his progress, submit reports to the Graduate Studies Committee and, finally, recommend for the degree.

The educational demands of the College require, in addition to the completion of satisfactory work in each of the studies pursued, that the student show capacity for independent work and for continued development in one or another field of knowledge.

Students who qualify for the degree of Master of Arts at Sarah Lawrence College will be eligible to continue graduate work in other universities. In general, the work for the degree may be completed in one academic year.

Students applying for admission to the Graduate Studies

16

Program of Sarah Lawrence College must have received the Bachelor of Arts degree from an accredited college or university. The College is interested in students who have a particular goal in seeking the Master's degree. For some students this period of study might constitute the first step toward the Doctor's degree, for others a final period of study before beginning to teach. For some it may serve as a preparation for other kinds of work related to their studies. In general, the Committee does not include in our limited number students who simply wish an extra year of study beyond the Bachelor of Arts degree.

The Committee on Graduate Studies judges each applicant by: (1) the undergraduate record, (2) a statement of purpose and goals of the candidate, (3) a personal interview, (4) the completion of a written form which will be sent to the candidate once the preliminary arrangements for application have been made. An interview with a member of the Committee or a regional representative will be arranged after the formal application has been accepted.

The start of the program: Facing the actualities of selecting students and planning programs

IN APRIL 1950, the *New York Times,* on its Sunday educational page, carried an announcement of the program of graduate studies to be offered at Sarah Lawrence College beginning in the fall of 1950. The leaflet containing the official statement about the program of graduate studies, with an accompanying letter, was sent to friends and acquaintances in other colleges by the President, the Dean, and interested members of the faculty. Inquiries began to come in from prospective students, and the Committee on Graduate Studies encountered its first unforeseen problem. Should all be allowed to go through with the full process of admissions or should there be some preliminary screening? If the letter from the applicant made clear that the specialized interest was one which could not be satisfied at Sarah Lawrence College, the matter could be easily handled in a reply suggesting other institutions noted for work in his field. Clear-cut cases such as these were few; in many instances the letters of inquiry were not sufficiently specific.

The experience of four years in admitting students to the graduate program has made several things clear. The desire for further

17

academic work among holders of the A.B. degree is wide-spread, the reasons are various, and the direction of this work only vaguely defined in the minds of the individuals. Previous assumptions that graduate students had found their direction, were strongly motivated, or "knew what they wanted," had to be given up. Again and again in interviews with applicants, especially those from large universities carrying extra numbers of students in recent years, applicants would say that they had had no opportunity in their undergraduate days to talk over plans for future studies. In other words, in the pressures on our educational system as a whole, advice to young men and women seeking careers in professions for which an M.A. is useful or required has not been given much attention. The strongly motivated student aspiring to the Ph.D. fares better. In its role as admissions officers, the Committee found itself engaged in personal counselling—to its surprise and consternation. The interview with the applicant became a major feature of the admission procedure.

An applicant may have an excellent undergraduate record and indicate in other ways the intellectual ability to do graduate work, but other factors not so readily ascertained have proved to be equally important. Since faculty at Sarah Lawrence College function both as teachers and advisers to undergraduates, the members of the Committee had had some experience in getting at underlying motives and in helping young people get started in directions for which their talents qualified them. Limited to a single interview with graduate applicants, the members of the Committee felt their own lack of experience and at first were inhibited by the general faculty attitude that graduate students were adults and should not be asked "personal" questions. Experiences in interviewing proved that potential graduate students, even those who were rejected, welcomed the chance to talk things over, and found the questions helpful in clarifying their own thinking.

Too many applicants who are about to receive the A.B., or who have been out of college a year or two, and still adrift, turn to the M.A. as a magic solution for their problems. Some think that teaching might be a pleasant way of life. They have given little consideration to what teaching involves or to their personal qualifications. Others hope that another year of study may help them decide what to do in the future. Individual applicants may not even be aware of their motivation or the lack of it. An interview, better than

18

any formal record, brings out relevant facts. Candidates for whom graduate study is suitable can be reassured about their decision. To others, for whom the study for the M.A. seems inappropriate, the Committee can suggest alternative plans in a friendly atmosphere. The Committee and the candidate are saved the wasteful process of completing an application which must end in rejection.

In considering the applicants for whom graduate work was appropriate, the Committee on Graduate Studies had also to consider, with as much objectivity as possible, whether the studies desired should be pursued at Sarah Lawrence. In the case of candidates whose major interest was in one of the arts or in nursery school education, clearly Sarah Lawrence had some special advantages to offer. But what about a candidate in the social sciences, literature, and languages, who might eventually wish to study for a Ph.D.? The answer in these cases could only be given on an individual basis. A graduate from a large university—a major in history, economics, philosophy, or literature—strongly attracted to teaching and giving some evidence of personal qualifications for the profession, might very well profit from a year of graduate work in a small college where he would have the experience of working on his own under the direction of a teacher who would have time to give to him. If his previous educational experience had been limited to large classes in a highly structured curriculum, the first year of work in a graduate school in which the Ph.D. is the main objective would be little more than another year of classes with too little opportunity to discover what independent study means. Some such candidates were accepted after the Committee made clear to the candidate the hazards involved in terms of recognition of the work by other graduate schools. Another group of candidates— young people who wished to round out or intensify their understanding of a chosen field preparatory to work in journalism, in research, in business, or in community organizations—could profit from work at Sarah Lawrence College, provided their chosen field was one in which we had teachers who were both qualified and interested in this advanced work.

In addition to the interview with the Committee, candidates who seemed to be good prospects were asked to meet with the teachers appropriate to their major interest. The teachers then conferred with the Committee and final acceptance rested on agreement of all concerned.

After the acceptance of a candidate, the Committee, the principal teacher, and the student undertake the formulation of a program of study. Ideally this should consist of what the candidate needs, in terms of what he brings with him and his immediate goal in studying for the M.A. Both the candidate and the principal teacher are likely to plan an impossible amount of work. The Committee must serve as a brake on these enthusiasms. This sounds simple, but it is not. In a college which has no required graduate courses, in which the relation between the various fields of knowledge is thought to be intimate, the principal teacher and the student are likely to take all knowledge for their province.

Since most of our candidates came from other colleges and universities where they had only had a limited experience as undergraduates in planning their education, the concept of creating a plan of studies within the limits of what they brought with them and their goal in qualifying for an M.A. was stimulating—rather heady wine for them. They needed guidance. The Committee had anticipated this need and allowed for frequent initial consultations between students, their principal teachers and others working with them, and the Committee, preparatory to getting down on paper a plan of work accepted by all concerned. The Committee had not, however, anticipated the need for continued reassurance about, or modification of, the initial program. During the first few months, both the teachers involved and the student needed the chance to evaluate the individual program.

More formal means of taking care of these matters seemed advisable. Individual members of the Committee became "readers" for two to three students; regular meetings with each student's teachers and the reader were scheduled. Students were advised to consult with the reader assigned to them about any of their problems.

The chief difficulty for graduate students who had had no previous experience in setting their own projects, and devising means of attaining results, was evidenced by their anxiety about what the College "expected of them." The idea of meeting their own expectations did not seem altogether legitimate. Actually what they were experiencing was the demanding business of satisfying both one's own requirements and the longing for limits imposed from without. This type of anxiety is evidence of a growing process and should not be too alarming to administrators; however, some aid must be

20

given in order that the anxiety not become too great. The readers were prepared to meet this type of anxiety since the faculty of Sarah Lawrence College have had experience with this in guiding juniors and seniors into independent work. The readers were not expecting to have to deal with graduate students about their personal problems. As a consequence, insufficient free time on the part of principal teachers and the Committee members made this kind of help difficult the first year. One reaction of the Committee of 1950-51 was that the questionnaire should contain more questions throwing light on the life situation of the candidates: family relations, finances, etc. The reader found himself acting as a guide in matters not directly connected with study, but matters which were interfering with the student's ability to make the most of his educational opportunity.

Defining the role of the Committee
on Graduate Studies in evaluating
the work of students

THE FUNCTIONS of the Committee in relation to teachers of graduate students assumed an unexpected prominence. Although programs had been accepted by the principal teacher and the Committee, other teachers who worked with graduate students sometimes became upset by what appeared to be a dual standard. They noticed that undergraduate seniors, working in the field of their major interest, often did better work than graduate students to whom the given field was of peripheral interest. The "ideal" graduate student should apparently excel in all areas. The anxiety of individual teachers trying to evaluate these two kinds of performance is understandable. Teachers accustomed to variations of achievement at the undergraduate level are likely to become panicky when the evaluation leads to an M.A. Some reverted to demands they had met in their traditional graduate training. Confronted with an actual student, who may have seemed less well-prepared for graduate work than the teacher involved thought proper, a number of questions about standards and expectations needed further consideration.

A qualitative judgment of what is happening in the teaching and learning process at any level makes great demands on the individual asked to give this judgment. The Committee realized that they needed to think about a number of things and to communicate their thinking to the faculty. Programs planned to meet the individual purposes of the candidate may include study in subjects conventionally classified as undergraduate. What proportion of a graduate student's time might legitimately and profitably be spent in full participation in an undergraduate course, when some understanding of this particular subject is obviously essential to the particular student? What, for the instructor of such a course, should be the criteria for evaluating the graduate student's work? In some disciplines, a ladder-like order of studies inheres in the subject matter; in others, the order is more in the nature of beginning at some point and moving out to the circumference. Subject matter in and of itself is not necessarily beginning or advanced. For graduate work the test is the use being made of the subject, the maturity of approach, and the relation of the study to the total program.

For teachers to formulate standards for evaluation of the student's work in his major interest is not so difficult as to set up standards for the graduate student in an undergraduate course. The Committee needed to help clarify the situation in each case for the teacher whose subject represented a secondary interest. For example, a candidate who had been a successful teacher of English in a private secondary school for three years, after her graduation from one of the larger women's colleges in the East, had been recommended by the principal of the school as especially gifted in establishing friendly relations with students in the junior and senior classes. This candidate had had only a single required course in psychology. She expressed a desire to take a course in *Psychology of Personality* (an advanced course at Sarah Lawrence College for undergraduates). Her theoretical knowledge in this area of psychology was less than the undergraduates in the course. This fact caused the instructor some concern. The reader from the Committee on Graduate Studies called a meeting of all the teachers working with this particular student to discuss the situation. The instructor in psychology became clearer in his mind about the use of this "undergraduate" work for a student primarily interested in literature, who would return to a teaching situation in which she would be permitted to choose the books to be read by girls from the ages of 15 to 18. It ceased to trouble the teacher that this particular student had read less of the literature of his subject than

22

undergraduate students who were primarily interested in psychology, and he gradually adopted a more flexible standard—a standard related to the quality of her work and the maturity with which she could handle the subject matter of the class.

With the limited number of graduate students, working in different areas and consequently with different teachers from year to year, the defining and interpreting function of successive members of the Committee with individual teachers has remained a continuing process.

In the second year of the program, the Committee held a series of meetings with faculty groups in which questions about qualifications of candidates in particular fields were raised. In each instance, after such a discussion, the group was asked to present in writing a set of minimal requirements for graduate work in their subject, to indicate if possible what types of students they could and would like to work with, and to give any other information that would be valuable to the Committee in responding to inquiries. For some groups or individuals this had still to be on an ideal basis, since no candidate in the first year had worked in their subject. Nevertheless, the formulation of these minimal requirements was of value both to the Committee and to the faculty.

Throughout the four years in which the Program of Graduate Studies has been offered, the Committee has found that a weekly meeting as a committee is essential for the discussion of policies, the making of plans to avoid mistakes that inevitably occur in an experimental situation, the carrying out of routine work involving the admission of students, the supervision of the work currently going on, the planning of ways of helping the handful of graduate students to feel at home in the College, and the consideration of means of attracting good candidates for the following year. In addition to these weekly meetings, individual members of the Committee meet regularly with the teachers of each student in the capacity of a "reader"; that is, as a member of the Committee who is supposed to know how the work is progressing and what social or personal needs are apparent for the students for whom the reader takes responsibility. The reader serves as an intermediary between the principal teacher and the student if that need arises. Students are urged to consult with their reader or the Dean, but many of the students, unused to this informal approach, were reluctant to "bother" the Dean, their teacher, or a Committee member with

23

their problems, so the Committee decided that the reader should initiate some conferences just to be sure that all was going well.

The final decision to recommend the granting of the M.A. rests with the Committee on Graduate Studies. These decisions are based on the following information: notes in writing from the reader about any informal meetings with the candidate, the teachers, or with both; written reports from teachers to the Committee around the middle of December, and at the end of January and April; written reports sent to students at mid-term; and final reports of teachers embodying an evaluation of work throughout the year. If the plan for the student included a written thesis, opinions of appropriate members of the faculty who have not worked with the student are secured. The decision of the Committee is first communicated to the principal teacher. In any case of a difference in opinion, the principal teachers and other teachers of the student in question are invited to confer with the Committee before the final recommendation is submitted.

The duties of a central committee responsible for a graduate program in any college are varied and exacting. In a small college undertaking a program for a properly limited number of candidates, there are great advantages in having the graduate work focused in a single committee. Departmental rivalry and variations in standards and requirements are avoided. The central committee can provide continuity from year to year. A plan by which one member goes off yearly and is replaced by another maintains a healthy circulation of interest in the program among the faculty. The committee builds up a body of knowledge and experience which helps it function more effectively in admissions, in planning individual programs, in assisting teachers and students in carrying out programs, and in evaluating the results.

CHAPTER TWO

Meeting the Problems of Graduate Study

ESTHER RAUSHENBUSH

THIS STUDY of a small graduate program is an account of how the educational philosophy and practices developed in the undergraduate program at Sarah Lawrence College have been applied to the problem of planning a first year of graduate study. It is the story of how first-year graduate students, seeking a Master of Arts degree, have been served by the individual planning, the absence of group or general requirements, the opportunity for seminar and conference discussions, and the counselling which are characteristic of the undergraduate college. The study of this special case can also give insight into the problems that any M.A. program is certain to have, whether it is large or small, and whether or not the administrators, teachers, and students are aware the problems exist.

This chapter will describe our efforts to discover what we need to know about students before we accept them, so that we can select candidates with a fair chance of being successful with them; and to set goals that are reasonable for them and that we can also respect as appropriate for graduate study. It will describe our effort to take into account both the talents and the limitations of our students in making individual plans for them.

In undertaking our M.A. program we were guided by the view that the system by which education in the undergraduate college is organized would be appropriate for first-year graduate students. Since the College and the program would always be small, it was not necessary to make plans that would fit large groups of students. It was possible to make individual plans for the graduate as we did for the undergraduate students. We were not limited by departmental requirements, but were free to set requirements that seemed appropriate in each case. The College could not, and did not wish to, set up a program of graduate courses; and did not need to since the tutorial conferences which form a very important part of the undergraduate program could be readily adapted to the needs of graduate students. The College had had nearly twenty-five years of experience in planning individually for the education of undergraduates. This procedure, useful and important for them, seemed to us at least as important for first-year graduate students. This opportunity is just as important for a student who is very clear about his goals as it is for one who has a general idea of what he wants to do, but who needs direction. Students embarking on graduate study often find gaps in their undergraduate education which must be remedied before they can continue their planned study; and the opportunity we offer for individual study and conference work makes it possible for them to do this without being seriously diverted from their goals. We have sometimes accepted good applicants who did not have a standard preparation, and who might have been rejected at another college; we are geared to making the special plans such a student needs. Not only is the student's program individually planned, but his intellectual and personal progress is followed through the year.

The undergraduate program at Sarah Lawrence College has a highly organized advising system in which each faculty member acts as adviser or "don" to a small number of students. The don meets at least once every two weeks for a conference with each student under his charge, keeps in touch with her progress at college, and is available for counsel and help on any matter, academic or personal, on which she seeks his advice. Counselling, therefore, is directed toward helping undergraduate students with their total college life, their adjustment to working and living at the College, the planning of the educational programs, and their progress toward the degree and toward life after college. We make no separation between academic and other counselling.

In originally planning the graduate program we agreed that we would not have such an advising system for the graduate students. We made this decision on the assumption that they were mature enough to deal with the ordering of their lives and that our responsibility to them was limited to their academic study as such. When we began working, it became clear that what was true for undergraduates was true also for them—we have found it impossible to ignore the problems of personal adjustment that rise to

26

plague both students and teachers, the problems of adjustment to the ways of working at this College, and the questions about goals.

In many instances the goals students have are vague and only partially defined, however dearly held; and the achievement of a college degree often leaves a quite-talented person still so deeply involved in making personal decisions that the involvement affects daily the academic work he is carrying on as a graduate student. As to the first of these difficulties, we have taken it as one of our tasks to help students define more precisely what they are looking for in doing graduate work at all and, in most cases, to follow a sharply defined plan for approaching the goal. As to the second, while we do not consider the solution of general life problems is part of our educational task, we have had to face realistically the fact that discussions of academic plans and academic work with students, or among the teachers of a particular student, often have to take account of personal problems and preoccupations. These very preoccupations may figure seriously in the actual making of plans, as the summary histories of students in the next chapter will indicate. Though we have not introduced a "donning" system paralleling that in the undergraduate college, we have abandoned the idea that we can deal exclusively with the graduate student's intellectual life any more than with the undergraduate's; and we have tried, through counselling by the principal teacher, and planning by the Committee on Graduate Studies, to take the total needs of these students into account.

This chapter will also give an account of the fields in which the graduate students worked, how we discovered in which areas we could really work with competence and style, and the variety of ways in which we have been successful and unsuccessful with students in different fields. This story of our success and failure may be thought to bear on our situation but not on others, because we have a range of possible studies, a faculty, an educational design, which is not duplicated exactly in another institution. In this sense everybody's experience is unique. But the connections between what we have, what we tried to do, and what we succeeded in doing should be relevant to the thinking of other people in other situations. Our most important task was one common to all colleges with such programs—to use the resources of the College as fully as possible to meet the goals of the students. We also point out here the assets and liabilities for graduate students of a program which teaches only a few graduate students in an undergraduate college. The values and problems of the Sarah Lawrence program may also exist in other small college graduate programs; and a discussion of our successes and failures may be useful to other people interested in such programs.

In selecting students for this program we have given preference to students from outside Sarah Lawrence College, and in fact have accepted our own graduates only when there seemed to us to be a compelling reason. We feel that a student who has spent four years here will gain important new experience in a year in another kind of institution. On the other hand, we believe that a year of study here based on the kind of planning we require could be very useful to a student from another kind of college or from a large university, especially a student who expects to teach. One reason is that our discussion classes and our conferences give the prospective teacher valuable experience for teaching. By way of exception, we have, in some instances, accepted applicants who had not spent all four undergraduate years at Sarah Lawrence, transfer students who had come to us as juniors; and in some instances Sarah Lawrence graduates have returned after several years to take the Master's degree. Most of our students, however, continue to be from other institutions, and this practice has enabled us to include both men and women in the program.

In all instances we have considered most carefully the motivation of the students applying. We have not been interested in students who are just seeking another year of study—an attitude that is acceptable in someone applying for admission to the undergraduate college but not on the graduate level. We have in fact tried to select students who have some very particular purpose, either immediate or in the forseeable future, in seeking a Master's degree. Good undergraduate grades alone are not adequate indication of purposefulness; many students get good grades in college while going through their studies in a perfectly routine fashion and without developing any particular motivation for study.

Among the highly motivated and correspondingly successful students are those who expect to continue for the Ph.D. and to prepare to teach in colleges. Such students who have come to us have sought out this College as a place where they could get a good first year of training toward their profession, and could also have an opportunity to observe, discuss, and work in a unique teaching environment. Three of the men who were in our graduate program during the first four years belong in this group, and after taking the M.A. they proceeded with their work for the Ph.D.

The flexibility that is the nature of the Sarah Lawrence program and ways of teaching makes it possible for us to relate a student's program to his goal quite directly; and to make it possible for him to shift it if, in the course of the year, new possibilities or new directions develop.

One young man (see the study of Frank Marsh in Chapter Three) was accepted as a student of theatre—he wanted to work in the theatre and to teach dramatics. Actually his talents lay in group work with young people, and we were able to plan a program for him which gave him a chance to use his talents in the theatre as an instrument for working with them. Had he understood his own goals better he might, perhaps, have gone to a school of social work instead of to Sarah Lawrence for his graduate degree, but with good work in the theatre available, a psychology faculty oriented toward developmental and personality psychology, and a member of that faculty as his main teacher who was also a trained social worker, it was possible to work out a very constructive graduate year for this young man, and to direct him toward a career which he is now successfully pursuing.

The variety of studies possible even in a small institution is very great when the system permits individual planning; students who are in the same general field but who have diverse purposes can make quite different plans, suitable to their individual needs. In the field of child development we have designed programs for students who come with a good deal of practical teaching experience but little theoretical knowledge, and who wish to understand children better in order to be better teachers; for foreign students who need to study not only American educational methods, but American mores, parent-child relations, and American institutions; and for students whose study of education and of children has been highly theoretical and who need the kind of combination of academic study and laboratory experience we have been able to give them—even for one student with a good deal of study in the field of psychoanalysis behind her whose goal was to write stories of mythology for children, and who stayed to be trained for research in child development.

Selecting the right students

IN THE short time our program has been in effect we have learned a good deal about how to ask the right questions of candidates for admission. We had to learn to ask the "right" questions because we rejected the assumption often made that graduate students should be accepted on the basis of academic criteria only, after which they are on their own. Whether the program is suited to them, whether they make the right choices within the program, whether the objectives they have set are appropriate for them or not, whether they can do the work or not, whether the work required of them is the most appropriate for their needs or not—these matters are often said to be the student's business, not the institution's. Our view has been (and it seems to us it should be the view of any small program) that none of us—institutions, faculty, nor students—can afford the dreadful waste that results from students getting into the wrong programs, struggling along for a while, and dropping out. It is pointless to say that it is their hard luck—it is everybody's hard luck. Perhaps it cannot be avoided in a graduate school that awards two hundred Master of Arts degrees in literature each year, but it should certainly be avoided in a program that grants ten or twenty M.A.s altogether.

One of the ways in which we try to avoid casualties is by not taking students who seem to have only an unformed notion that it would be a good idea to have an advanced degree. This does not, of course, mean that the beginning graduate student can be expected to be certain both about the exact character of the professional goal he seeks and about his ability to achieve it. In fact, some of our most successful graduate students have been those whose work at Sarah Lawrence led them directly, and as a result of our planning with them, to work or further study which they had not in the least anticipated.

One interesting and difficult case was that of a student who came as a student of painting. We were not able to judge her competence well enough, soon enough, to plan the best kind of program for her. We knew she wanted to teach painting, preferably in a college art department, but possibly in a secondary school. Had we continued to consider her a student of painting, as we did in the beginning, we would have failed to prepare her for the kind of teaching for which she really did have talent. She was not a gifted painter, and in that sense not a good student of painting, but she was a very good student of the history of art, of aesthetics, and of philosophy, and on taking her degree was appointed to teach history of art in a college having very high teaching standards.

Another student came to us because he was interested in community problems; he knew we had worked a good deal in this area, and he hoped to take a degree in sociology, working principally on some aspects of the theory of community organization. The kind of sociological study he thought he wanted to do, and that we thought appropriate, he had neither the training nor the intellectual drive to do. As a subordinate part of the original plan we had set up a field-work project for him that required his presence in the field a good many hours a week. He soon demonstrated that while he could not deal with the theoretical problems involved in the original plan, he did have a good deal of talent for actual work in the field, for making important observations, for imaginative analysis of community organization, and for dealing in terms of action with the problems he met. We shifted his program so that the major emphasis was on field study; work in this area was certainly important, he needed the training we could give him, and he was able to do good work in this field. Instead of a theoretical essay on community organization he wrote as a Master's essay an excellent analysis of certain significant minority issues in the community he studied. Had we allowed him to continue according to the original plan he would have failed to get his degree; had we pointed out his shortcomings but offered no appropriate alternative he would have left the program after the first few months. The shifting of his goals and his program both set him on a constructive path for his life work and made it possible for us to guide him to a creative year of work instead of one that would be destructive, or at least meaningless; and to a respectable Master's degree. We lost some time in the process, but a few instances of this kind taught us what questions to ask to discover whether the candidate has the qualities necessary for the pursuit of the purposes for which he comes. We came to be more secure in rejecting a candidate on the grounds that his plan for study is inappropriate, and also more ready to place particular conditions on the work of a particular student.

We have felt that we can afford to take some calculated risks in accepting students, since we have an opportunity to work closely with them and are prepared to shift programs and seek other ways of making the year's study a good one. We have, for instance, several times accepted students with rather unusual training, on the chance that we would be able to work out with them ways of combining this training with work available at the College in the interest of a particular goal. In one instance we accepted a student who had worked in the Jungian Institute for several years, although not under a very systematic program. She came interested in studying myth for the purpose of learning how to use mythological materials in writing for children. We discovered that practically all her work relating to children had been of a theoretical nature, and that she had had no experience at all with live children. This became evident as she began her studies, and her program was revised to allow for a good deal of work in the nursery school under the supervision of the teachers in the field of child development. She developed an aptitude for work with children, although her intellectual interests and temperament caused her to lean toward research. After completing her work here she entered a research institute in child development at one of our large universities, where she is working in a field certainly different from the one she originally had in mind, but using the talents and experience she brought from her earlier experience.

For all our willingness to be flexible we cannot allow a student to undertake a program which, while within her competence and interest, is not educationally sound in our terms. Our convictions about what kind of education is justifiable in terms of the philosophy and the educational objectives of the College make it important for us to select students whose ability and training will enable us to plan programs that are acceptable to us as well as suitable for them. The fact that we do not have a prefabricated program into which students must fit, and expectations as to subject matter and ways of working that they can read in the Catalogue, means that we need to take greater precautions than we otherwise would against admitting the wrong students.

In the first year of our program we accepted a student who wanted to become a high school teacher of mathematics. We accepted her because we were interested in potential high school teachers, and had in our faculty some strong convictions about how mathematics should be taught. We had tried to carry out these views in our undergraduate classes and felt that a student wishing to teach could develop an acceptable attitude toward the teaching of mathematics from her experience here. Too much teaching of mathematics in schools, and in many colleges as well, is the teaching of formulae, the discipline of memorizing, the solving of problems; too little has to do with the development and analysis of principles. This student came with good undergraduate grades, and we thought we had a chance here of sending a liberally trained young teacher on her way. We soon found that this student had skill in solving problems but no interest in, and no capacity for, dealing with general principles. She was ill at ease with us. She knew a way of going about mathematics that suited her, and the aspect of this study that seemed most important to us seemed least so to her. We came to feel that if she were to become any kind of high school teacher of mathematics it would be the kind of teacher she had herself been taught by as an undergraduate, and would approach the study as her teachers approached it. We were not willing to give a degree for the development of such skills alone. We encouraged her, since she sought the teaching certificate, not to work for an M.A. that year but to make the year a profitable one by taking such studies as would help her toward certification, and to study mathematics later in an environment more congenial to her. This she was unwilling to do, and she left the College when the year was half over.

The experience of this student and several others brought home to us the futility of setting up a program for a student which, although it is calculated to achieve something we value educationally, is inappropriate for the student we have to teach. This student suffered not only from her own inadequacies but from our unrealistic expectations for her. What would have been quite suitable for another student was meaningless for her—though in another kind of program she might have met the requirements and taken the degree.

Our admissions procedures of our first years failed us in a few other cases too, each of which has, to be sure, been useful in helping us discover what kinds of information we need to obtain from students in application materials and in interviews, to help us make the right judgments. Another error we made the first year was to admit a student who said she wanted to teach painting in schools. She had graduated from Sarah Lawrence College two years earlier. We rarely admit Sarah Lawrence graduates, and we know now that we should not have admitted this one. As an undergraduate she had worked several years with a painter on our faculty, and we now think that she wanted a year more of painting with him, and not a year of graduate study. With the perspective we have gained, we would now be able to protect both her and ourselves against the mistake of admitting her.

Another kind of difficulty, found in any educational program, is the problem of dealing with psychologically disturbed students. It must happen frequently in graduate schools that such students begin study and have to drop out; and in big programs, often no one knows why. In a program where there are fewer students it should be possible to make some judgments about emotional stability and to protect both the student and the institution from the waste of time, energy, and money caused by such misjudgments. Our procedures the first year failed to disclose signs of quite severe psychological disturbance in an able student who found it impossible to attend to her studies at all. We were able to direct this student to psychotherapy, so that the truncated experience here was probably not altogether lost.

We have each year a number of applications from married women, out of college for some years, who want to continue their studies. Some of these are apparently seeking a way of using time that is personally satisfying to them; others, young married women who have not begun their families, are thinking ahead to possible work in the future; others, out of a desire to work or a need to earn money, want to prepare for immediate jobs. In the case of these women, too, we need to guard against inadequate motivation. It is not enough that they would "like to study," and it is important to distinguish between those who are able to accept the discipline of a graduate program and those who really want a kind of adult education study. One student we accepted was a highly intelligent woman, interested in ideas, and with a lively curiosity. She had quite an elaborate domestic establishment, with the kind of service and economic security that might seem to make the prospect for serious study by a serious-minded person quite good. But the social demands of her life intruded continually on her work; apparently we had misjudged the motivation for work, which turned out not to be strong enough to make a reorganization of her personal life possible, and we advised her to drop out.

On the whole, the record of the young married women in our

program is a very good one. Obviously, no planning can guard against sudden contingencies—illness in the family, a shift in a husband's business career, the birth of a child—but we are better able now to make judgments about which women with family responsibilities are most likely to be able to carry their plans for study through successfully. The main factor, in predicting success, granted competence to begin with, is, as always, the kind and amount of motivation a student has. There is no doubt that a professional motivation is the strongest among those that bring married women into graduate programs; and, obviously, the more immediate the need, the more single-mindedness goes into the study. When the need for undertaking professional work is urgent, the program is more sharply directed (and in some instances narrower) than it otherwise would be.

Several of our married women students were eager to finish their work as well as they could in the shortest possible time, in order to qualify for teaching. Several others, not confronted with the immediate need for winning financial security, who, however, also hope to teach at some time, were able to plan somewhat more leisurely, more general programs. The former group press for programs that would give them as much specific material as possible for teaching; the latter give themselves an opportunity to undertake research projects, learn how to do more scholarly studies, and increase their general knowledge of their field.

One student, married and the mother of four children, could allow herself just one year of graduate study before moving with her family to a rural home in New England where she planned to teach school. Her need was to qualify for a position in a high school teaching social studies; she particularly needed a good program of work in American history. Her ability and motivation, and the cooperation of her family, all supported the year of graduate study. A second student, a good many years out of college, who was confronted with the need to work and who was interested in teaching, undertook a program directed toward certification and the Master's degree as well. With a child to care for, and without the resources of the first student, she worked steadily in a two-year program which prepared her for a profession for which she has talent and which she can follow while she brings up her child. Her work was principally in psychology and in child development, and she was able to carry on her studies in the College and also have a valuable practice teaching experience that was carefully integrated into her more theoretical studies.

We have had a number of such students in our program. They have done very well, and the experience of teaching them contrasts happily with the frustration we all experienced trying to work with the first one described here. Most of the married women who apply to us wish to teach, and in interviewing them we feel it important to learn as much as we can about their family situations in order to discourage those who, perhaps not visualizing the complexities, are attempting a task that is beyond them, and to admit those whose expectations are reasonable and for whom we can plan good programs. College grades give us little light, beyond an indication of intellectual competence. The factors that count most, granted adequate ability, are harder to recognize, and certainly a large program could do little to seek them out. It is one of the advantages of a small program that a serious effort can be made to spare the waste of an unconsidered attempt to carry on graduate study.

This influx of graduate students who have been out of college from two to ten years was unexpected. We had originally planned our program for students just out of college; and when the applications from married students began coming in our inclination was not to accept them, especially after one or two unhappy experiences with people too subject to other pressures. Since then, however, we have found them to be among the most serious and rewarding students, if they are properly selected—women who will make good use of their experience here in many ways, and particularly in teaching.

A comparison of the records of the students accepted during each of the first four years of the program corroborates the impression that the Committee gained a good deal of skill in selecting students who are likely to succeed in their studies and for whom our kind of flexible program is a good one, and also that the Committee grew more knowing about planning for them. Of the eight students we had the first year of the program, three were excellent candidates for the kind of graduate study we were able to provide. Of these, one was well prepared in the field of nursery education to move toward a nursery school directorship; another worked in American studies and then took a position in which he directly used his studies; the third has completed his doctorate, and is teaching. Three were students (all women) whose purposes were unclear, whose motivation was doubtful, and who were unable to complete the year of study. Their academic records had looked good, our interviews failed to discover the difficulties which, after they were brought out in the work, seemed obvious to all of us. A seventh student would probably have worked better and with much less anxiety in a program that developed particular skills but did not ask of her the kind of theoretical thinking we asked of her. The eighth, already described, came presumably to prepare for teaching but actually for a year more of painting; although she went through the motions, she gained little from her year in terms of our conceptions.

By the end of the first year we were much more aware of the problems of admission and planning. In the second year we were able to avoid some of the pitfalls. The third and fourth years were even better; among the seventeen students we accepted only two were unable to complete their work, and all the others worked on a level very satisfactory to the Committee. Of the two who failed to complete their work, one was unclear about her purposes, had many conflicting demands on her time, and was able neither to clarify her purpose nor manage the interferences. The other was an art student who came with the apparent intention of preparing for teaching in the public schools but who was unable to accept the requirements necessary for that kind of study. With a few students there were difficulties in limiting or defining their goals for the degree; each of them presented the problem of carving out a program suited to his particular experience and education, and to his qualities and the purposes for which the degree was sought. One student had a problem of both physical and emotional health to cope with. In every other instance, during these two years, good decisions were made by the Committee, the students were able to meet the requirements set, and the programs were suitable to their purposes.

Finding the fields in which we work best with students

IN PLANNING the program originally we did not decide that we would offer the degree in certain fields and not in others. The curriculum of the College is roughly divided into four areas: the social sciences, literature and languages, the natural sciences, and the arts. Undergraduates do not have to declare a major; and although the records of almost all indicate that they have a major of sorts, this has grown out of the considerations in planning for the student rather than out of any stated content of a "major" program. There are no general subject-matter requirements for the undergraduates. With this point of view as part of the design of the College, we worked with the background, aptitudes, and objectives of each candidate for the M.A. and did not set up a program of general subject-matter requirements, either for all candidates, or for all candidates in a given field.

There were, however, a number of considerations in planning for graduate students that did not apply to the undergraduates. It was said earlier that we learned to seek a fairly well-defined objective in our M.A. candidates. This is not, of course, asked of undergraduates. Undergraduate years, for some students, are largely exploring and developing years not directed toward a practical goal. We were, then, committed to make plans for graduate students, not solely in terms of their general educational needs, but in these more specific terms as well. Over the years, we have developed an undergraduate program that is unusually varied for a small college in the four areas indicated. It has taken the experience of making plans with graduate applicants to discover in which areas to accept graduate students. In those fields in which we are perhaps better able to offer work than some other institutions, the kind of individual planning we have followed has resulted in very diverse programs.

In deciding which applicants to accept, we have had to consider both the plans of the applicant and the facilities of the College. The discussions between the Committee on Graduate Studies and members of the faculty in various fields which helped us make these decisions have been described in the first chapter.

The work possible here in the social sciences, particularly in American studies, has provided the basis for good graduate programs; the work in American history and the history of ideas, in government, economics, philosophy and social philosophy forms an important aspect of the undergraduate program. A seminar in *Ideas in America* for advanced undergraduate students in this field has been especially useful for students with an undergraduate background in American history, and for foreign students expecting to teach American history or literature in their own countries.

We could, with our experience in field work, do much more than we have yet done in planning graduate programs directed toward community studies. Since the program began we have had only one student in this field, which has very great possibilities for prospective teachers of the social sciences, and people interested in group or community work of various kinds who are not interested in a professional social work training.

We are very much interested in the possibility of working with students in international relations and international economics, and the interests and training of several of our faculty members make possible excellent graduate study in these fields for students prepared for it in undergraduate work. However, since most students interested in this field come to their graduate work with less preparation for it than for certain other fields, a single year of graduate study cannot take them as far, ordinarily, as study in the American field can. In specialized area studies we are, naturally, limited, although we do offer undergraduate studies in Southeast Asia, Italian and Russian history, contemporary Russia, and Russian literature.

Our undergraduate program in the performing arts has had an important place in our curriculum, and we have had many years of experience in planning good educational programs for students interested in dance, in giving them a variety of experiences in the performing arts, and in teaching them to use their knowledge in other fields in the service of their work in composition and in choreography. A graduate degree in this field is becoming more important each year as more colleges include dance in their programs, and teaching becomes an important way for an educated dancer to use her talents.

We have also for many years had a program in the field of child development, and many of our graduates went into nursery school work before we had a Certification Program or a Graduate Studies Program. Like the dance program, this one has been important in the Graduate Studies Program because of the experience we had already accumulated in planning a good general education for the girl interested in this field.

Many colleges have small graduate study programs centered in the sciences, which give students the opportunity to take a graduate degree and at the same time act as assistants in science. Since this kind of work-study combination is more common in science than elsewhere, a number of colleges limit their degrees to this field. The plan has advantages for the student in giving her an opportunity to study, and at the same time both the chance to earn part of her graduate studies' expenses and the experience to do work in her field. We have not offered this kind of plan. Our classes are small, students work closely with the instructors, and while there is need for assistance in handling apparatus, for instance, the actual laboratory teaching is done by the regular instructors.

We have thus not had this means for attracting science students, and for this and other reasons have not yet developed a program for a graduate year in science. We have experimented a good deal with the undergraduate teaching of the biological sciences, and we believe that this program is peculiarly suited to the training of prospective high school teachers of biology. This is one of the fields in which we need to do further exploring, and in which we should have something to offer which we have not yet worked out.

Programs for students planning to teach

IN VARIETY and range, the experience that students have who come to us wishing to prepare for teaching has been very great—students have gone from here to teach on all levels from the nursery school to college, and, considering our small numbers, in an interesting variety of fields.

A graduate of the University of Copenhagen who had already begun her teaching career in a Folks School in Denmark, came to take a degree in the field of American studies. (See the summary of Karen Rosencrantz in Chapter Three). She was then teaching and planned to continue to teach American literature in her own country. Her knowledge of continental literature was quite good— better than her knowledge of American literature. The direction for the work of such a student was quite clear, the planning of a suitable program not a difficult task, and working with her a pleasure. She took an intermediate course called *American Life and Thought* which broadened her conception of how American materials could be used with undergraduate American students; and she took a seminar called *Ideas in America* which gave her an opportunity to work on special problems in the field of American social history as a background for her studies in literature. We felt

40

that for the first semester of her stay here it was important to give her this kind of background for understanding American literature. At the same time she did certain reading in European literature that has been important for its influence on American literature. Most of her time the second semester was spent in reading American literature, and this included a good deal of nineteenth century background and the intensive study of one contemporary writer— William Faulkner.

Another young woman with experience as a teacher of English in a private school entered the program wanting a year of directed study to improve her knowledge of literature and her understanding as a critic. It was quite clear, not only from the information we had about her, but from discussion with her, that she was a natural teacher, liked young people, and liked working with them. But she needed both range and the chance to use her imagination in her own reading and study, and some surer understanding of the age-group she worked with. For this student, a combination of general reading and an intensive project leading to a thesis in literature seemed indicated, and a substantial course in psychology emphasizing the psychology of adolescence seemed appropriate. She did most of her work in literature on a tutorial basis, reading widely, writing critical papers, and also working on a Master's essay on the novels of Virginia Woolf. Her work in psychology was done principally in an advanced undergraduate course in that field, with tutorial readings. The literature teacher with whom she studied gave her several opportunities to take over one of her classes, so that she had a number of good teaching experiences as well.

Dance students planning to teach: We have had a very gratifying experience in working with graduate students in dance. Our College program is a good one for this purpose because our undergraduate teaching of dance has full academic status, and is not a branch of the physical education program. Nor is it a program designed for specialists, but rather a very solid program with the range and substance of work found in any other art, science, or social science. It is taught as part of our general liberal arts program, combining work in dance technique, choreography, and composition with work in design, music for dance, reading, and seminar studies; and it is directed toward the education of college students generally.

The graduate students who enter this program, however, are,

or want to become specialists. But since they all want to teach dance, most of them in colleges, they have an unusually good opportunity to work in a highly developed undergraduate program which gives them excellent training for working in their own future college programs. They have college students, beginners and others, actually to work among and work with. They are most likely to—and most of them do—get teaching posts in colleges with the Master's degree, and work, in many instances, in expanding programs, since dance programs are becoming more important in many colleges.

In the first year of the program we had only one dance student, and only one the second year; in the third there were four, of whom one remained for two years, and two new ones in the fourth year.

As the summary of the experience of Joan Brent (see Chapter Three) indicates, while she worked in dance during her year here, much of her study was in poetry and anthropology, and she audited a literature course, *The Artist in Modern Society*. She had regular weekly conferences on the teaching of dance in college, with the dance director, and toward the end of her year had an opportunity to teach two periods weekly in movement. Her study of poetry was the basis of her major work in dance for the degree, a large section of a dance program for which she was to do the choreography for groups of dancers and in which she was to compose a solo dance. The problem set was the use of spoken words as an accompaniment or as an intrinsic part of dance composition. She also composed and danced a solo based on the legends of the Zuñi Indians, using material suggested by her work in anthropology.

The most important observation to make about this program, as it relates to our general planning for the Master's degree, is the fact that in a small and highly unified college like this one the teacher of poetry and the teacher of anthropology are able to work directly with a student on material for her choreography, and she is able to bring back to them a picture of her needs as a dancer which in turn makes it possible for them to help her with the material they know. Incidentally it might be remarked that this kind of experience is invaluable for the college teacher as well. In this instance it gave to the poet who taught the course in poetry an insight into the possible union of dance and poetry which was new in his creative experience.

One student of dance came on leave of absence from the dance department of a college, needing more experience in choreography and composition, and her program was planned with this in mind.

Another dance student had had a much livelier and fuller undergraduate program in a liberal arts college, and we felt that in most respects we did not need to supplement this as we did for the first student. Her studies in dance had been principally in a college program, and she had not had the kind of professional study the student described above had had. We thought she needed two things: to have a literature program that would give her some opportunity to learn something about the attitudes toward the arts, and the experience of art at least of a particular period in history; and to continue work in technique and choreography combined with related work in theatre and music that would add to her total experience as a dancer. In addition to her work in dance, she registered for a course in eighteenth-century literature, and a program of conference reading gave her an opportunity to learn a good deal about classical art in England and France, about the painting and music as well as the literature of the period. In the theatre she worked in an acting class, and with the technical director, learning a good deal about stage design, lighting, and the actual process of mounting a performance.

As a new college graduate, she was younger than most of the other dance students, who had taken time out, usually to earn money, before undertaking their graduate study, and it was arranged that she should take two years for the degree. Another important factor in her education was that she came saying she wanted to be a professional dancer, but was hoping to learn as much as she could from a year of graduate study and the environment of the College, about what possible uses there might be for her talents, since she had to support herself. Before the end of her second year it was clear that not the professional stage, but teaching, would be an appropriate goal for her, and she did, in fact, on completing her degree, take a position in a New York City college to teach dance.

This girl was a talented dancer who needed continuing work in dance, study in related fields, and the opportunity to work with other students, and to bring to some culmination on a fairly large scale her own creative work. She was reported by her faculty as an important contributor to the work of other and younger students by performing on a level the undergraduates could not reach, the

43

dances composed by other students. There were a number of talented students in choreography in the undergraduate group who could not have brought their work to the kind of finish it reached, had she not been there, and it gave her the chance to work at an aspect of dance which would be very useful to her as a teacher.

A fourth student had majored in sociology in a good undergraduate college and had always been interested in dance; she had completed her undergraduate studies with the hope of continuing her study of dance, preparing to teach dance and to continue with her own interest in choreography. Unlike the first student described above, she had not had the opportunity to study with professional groups, nor to work as an undergraduate in a college giving much opportunity to study in this field. Since she was attending a New York college, throughout her college career she was able to continue studying in settlement houses and semi-professional groups, to spend summers at the Colorado Summer School of the Dance, and to teach in a small group in the city. Our principal purpose with this girl was to give her an intensive experience in dance technique and choreography, and in design for the theatre as a way of encouraging especially her talents in choreography. She took a course, also, in *Folklore and Myth* which served to provide her, as work in anthropology and poetry had other students, with material for creating dances, and for extending her knowledge of how to use literary and other materials in teaching. This student, on completing her work, was appointed to a post teaching dance in a state university.

Students planning to teach in nursery schools: Child development and early childhood education have been among the most important areas of study for the Master's degree. The College has for many years had an excellent program of work in child study and developmental psychology—these were important areas of our curriculum even before we entered upon a program preparing undergraduates for nursery school teaching. They are important fields of study in a liberal arts education for many students, and it was for these purposes such courses were developed. Over the past ten years or so more and more of our students who undertook these studies have been sought as teachers in private nursery schools and kindergartens, and in 1950 Sarah Lawrence undertook a certification program for interested undergraduate students. This involved little change in our curriculum, since all students had in any case

44

as part of their general study in developmental psychology had a good deal of experience observing and teaching under supervision in our own nursery school and in the local public school. Work had been regularly offered in *Learning Theory, Child Development,* and related areas.

During the years the Graduate Studies Program has been in existence we have had a number of students in this field each year and a brief account of the different kinds of experience and need they brought to their study will indicate the importance of individually planned programs for such students.

One student who had worked in a good undergraduate program of child study wanted as much professional training as possible which would help prepare her for work as a nursery school director. For this student (at that time the only one with these goals in our program) we worked out a joint program with an excellent professional school that did not grant a degree but did have facilities for work in the administrative field. By this means, taking a year and a half for the degree, the student was able to get the kind of academic and theoretical studies possible at the College, and the rather specialized professional studies she needed elsewhere.

Another student was a Japanese girl, recently come to this country, with excellent academic training behind her, but with no knowledge of our schools, and our task with her was to plan a program that would give her as much experience as possible, both practical and theoretical, to aid her to understand American schools and American children.

A third student came to us with a good record in a rather specialized teacher-training school, and a good deal of practical experience with children (see the summary of Ivy Chase in Chapter Three.) She had studied *Curriculum Development and Practices, Educational Psychology,* and *Educational Methods,* and had had studies in the social sciences and in the biological sciences; but she had had very little study of dynamic psychology, of personality development, or, in fact, except in a limited way, of the growth and development of children. As the faculty member who worked with her on planning a program wrote, "She recognizes that her education has been somewhat turned around, and is seriously interested in doing something about this. I believe we can provide her with the opportunity to pull her experiences and ideas together, to take a breather, to learn the basis of some of the prac-

45

tices in teaching, and to think." This student's program included no systematic work in the nursery school, but was built mainly around a course in *Personality Development* in which the reading and discussion was related directly to her previous experiences with children in the school situation, together with related studies in literature.

Students planning to teach in other fields: As indicated above, the history of our students' interest in the social sciences is quite different from the history of the students in dance, for instance. Almost all the dance students moved directly from their graduate studies into teaching—principally into college teaching. Our students in child development also moved quite directly into teaching posts—mostly in nursery or elementary schools, a few into settlement houses or child-care centers. The students in the social sciences have been with a few exceptions men and women interested in gaining experience in the elements of research, and in going on to further study, probably with college teaching in mind.

Three of the students who worked in the field of American studies are described in Chapter Three—Mrs. Winston planning to teach in a high school, Jan Tesek studying here preparatory to continuing advanced studies elsewhere, and Karen Rosencrantz preparing to teach American literature in the Danish public schools. A fourth student who worked in American political philosophy here went on to further graduate study in philosophy and is now teaching, and another who studied philosophy in her Master's year here is continuing toward her Ph.D. with the expectation of returning to her home in Egypt to teach.

The adjustment of graduate students to the undergraduate College

ONE OF THE great advantages of a good graduate school, if it is not too large, or a graduate department, if it is made up of congenial people, is the companionship, both personal and working, that springs from the common purposes of the students in the program. In a very large graduate program these personal relations are sometimes lost, and it is possible for a graduate student in a great university to be very lonely and isolated, especially in his first year. But the chance for communication with others of one's own kind is there, and is very important. The absence of this in a small program is one of our serious drawbacks; and although most of our graduate students know, when they come, that they will be a very small group with very diverse interests, they miss the relations they want to have with other students. This is the problem most often mentioned when we ask students about their difficulties and dissatisfactions. It is likely that even in small institutions appointing graduate assistants to laboratory posts, or to other services bringing them in regular association with faculty members and undergraduates, the graduate students find a group to which they can belong. Here, however, a program may be planned for a graduate student that centers her work in tutorials with one or more faculty members, assigns her to an advanced undergraduate course, and, in the nature of the program, is able to provide no graduate group for her to join. This needs to be made clear to prospective candidates before they undertake to study in this situation. On the other hand, relations with the faculty are friendly and easy, and many students are glad to forfeit association with graduate students for the access they have to the faculty.

In some fields this is no problem. Graduate students in dance or theatre quickly become members of the group, which works together many hours weekly. Graduate students in dance work in technique classes with undergraduates, do choreography with them and for them, perform in dances composed by undergraduates, sometimes teach classes, and work on crews with undergraduates. In the nursery school, too, where prospective teachers do practice teaching, the distinctions break down, and good companionship between graduates, undergraduates, and faculty is common, and the feeling of isolation disappears. On the other hand, the student of history or literature, politics or psychology, is likely to be working alone much of the time and, if she cannot be happy associating with undergraduates, must find her companionship outside the College.

The foreign students: Our experience with foreign students in the Graduate Studies Program is naturally very brief. We have had five foreign students—one French, one English, two Indian, and one Danish. A recent study made under the auspices of the New York Council for Foreign Students points up many problems common to foreign students whatever institution they attend—homesickness, difficulties with housing, difficulties with language, with food, with money, difficulties in understanding the educational system, American standards and the level of education of American students, the routines of program planning and registration, the impersonality of advisers, and so on. Some of these present no problems to the students who come to us, but others are enhanced here. Faculty members in this College expect to work closely with students, are experienced in counselling, and are interested in adjustment problems of all students. Interested adults are not lacking to help ease the induction into American academic life. We have little trouble with language problems—we investigate as fully as possible the prospective student's knowledge of spoken as well as written English, and those who have come to us are fluent enough. On the other hand, the leap from any European university to any American university would be quite great; the leap from an European university to Sarah Lawrence is much greater, and the absence of familiar routines, such as the preparation for a crucial final examination, the combination of great freedom and flexibility in planning programs (which sometimes looks chaotic to them), and the regular supervision of studies through weekly tutorial conferences, is hard for some of them to understand, as is the absence of the high degree of specialization they often expect. The most successful foreign student is one who understands the character of the College and who seeks the kind of teaching offered here; who wants to study something which clearly can be studied better in America than in her home country, and which she feels can be studied best in this environment.

Most foreign students coming to this country seek scholarship aid, and take scholarships where they are offered, and for this reason it is very important for us to select carefully those for whom this will be likely to be a good environment. An English student who came here never became reconciled to our refusal to permit her to continue in her studies here the high degree of specialization she had undertaken at her home university; on the other hand, a Danish girl who came to America to study American history and literature deliberately chose this College because it was small, because she could study with particular professors whose work interested her, because she was interested to have for herself the experience of working in small classes and in conferences, and could learn here, by participating and observing, much that would help her in her own teaching when she returned home.

Such problems as are indicated here cannot be fully resolved.

48

In the case of foreign and American students alike it is even more important for the small college than for the large one, or the university, to choose carefully, seeking students who know what they want, understand the assets and liabilities of the program and the College, and who, for their needs, want what the College has to offer that cannot easily be found elsewhere.

CHAPTER THREE

The Experience of Seven Students

JANE G. JUDGE

A SUMMARY of all the study plans of the students who have
taken degrees under this program would survey the variety
and range of work which resulted from the kind of individual planning described in the preceding chapters. Such a survey could not,
however, give any picture of the continuing evaluation and re-
planning that can go into the shaping of a Master's degree program
created for a small number of students. For this reason the present
chapter undertakes to describe the experience of seven students, all
seeking to prepare for teaching (from nursery school to college
teaching), four expecting to end their formal study with the Master's degree, three expecting to continue for the Ph.D. These are all
students who had successful experiences; the records, however,
indicate typical difficulties which arose from the limitations of the
students' previous education, the limitations of the small-college
offerings, our inadequate understanding of what they knew and
what they needed, and the shifts in goals which sometimes take
place as a student becomes more and more involved in a program
which once seemed appropriate but which turns out not to be so.
The shifts in study plans that are possible in a situation like ours,
in which much of the work of the graduate student is on a tutorial
basis, cannot be made in a larger program; it is one of the compen-
sations for the absence of graduate courses and one of the assets
of a small program.

*Bridging the gap between college
and study for the Ph.D.*

JAN TESEK, a young American of European background, had
majored in history at a large midwestern university. He applied for
admission to the Master of Arts program in American history,

planning to continue his studies toward a Ph.D. in history with the ultimate objective of teaching history on a college level. He had a reading knowledge of French and German and was relearning his native language, Czech, through independent study.

In his application form he stated:

> I've chosen the graduate program at Sarah Lawrence College because I think that it would best fulfill those standards of education which I learned to appreciate at X college.

Prior to his transfer in his junior year to a university, he had studied at a small college based upon the principle of small discussion classes and the tutorial system of instruction.

> I have been inquiring about graduate schools for some time and have had the chance to see one in action at Y university. I have been generally dissatisfied with the prospects of large lecture halls and overcrowded seminars. I heard about Sarah Lawrence through a graduate student who is familiar with the college, and I have read *Essays in Teaching,* edited by Dr. Taylor. I am familiar with the works of several scholars at Sarah Lawrence who strike me as outstanding figures in the field of Social Science.

He was recommended by his university as a conscientious, hard working, thoughtful student, genuinely interested in scholarship, who should be able to do very satisfactory graduate work, at both the M.A. and later the Ph.D. level. The original program planned for Jan consisted of:

1. *Research Conference on 19th Century Immigration to the United States:* Research on problems of acculturation of Czech immigrants to the United States. Born and brought up through childhood in Czechoslovakia, he had more than academic interest in this problem.
2. *19th Century German Philosophy:* An advanced course in which he was expected to do both class and individual conference work.
3. Attendance at a seminar on *Ideas in America.*

His experience both with his original research project and with his study of philosophy illustrates the advantages of flexibility in such a program. A careful examination of the materials in the New York Public Library and other large libraries, and consultation with Czechs in the New York area, forced him to the conclusion that there was as yet too little material available to him on this subject to warrant even a brief study. He learned a great deal, as students do, from this abortive search for materials, and wrote up his experience in a brief report. Ordinarily, in beginning research training it is necessary for students to undertake a "safe" project, since time is limited. It was useful to this student, both for the experience itself, and for his future interest in the original subject, in which he has an intellectual and emotional investment, to be able to explore, and at the same time to have close enough supervision to be advised when to stop exploring to avoid wasting time. His general interest in the problem of acculturation, and in pursuing the method of study he had begun, led him instead to undertake a study of German immigrants from 1820-1890. For part of his study he used the writings of German travelers to America with the intention of discovering to what degree they confirmed conventional attitudes toward the role of the German immigrant in America, and what evidence they offered concerning immigrant and non-immigrant German ideas of America.

The course in *German Philosophy* had been decided on because it explored ideas which had conditioned the thinking of large numbers of immigrants not only from Germany, but from Central Europe to the United States. This course involved extended reading in original sources, and a few weeks of study made it clear that Jan's general background in philosophy was inadequate for the kind of study planned. It was decided that he should continue reading for general knowledge in this field in conferences with the teacher of philosophy, but that his principal reading program should be directed toward historical American studies related to his special topic, and *Studies in American Literature*. It was his plan to continue American studies generally, along with his interest in the problem of acculturation, to go on for a Ph.D., and eventually to teach American history.

This program he carried through the year, submitting at the end of the year a thesis on "The German Immigrant and his Image of the United States, 1848-54, 1880-86."

In evaluating his study for the period to December, Jan writes:

52

My work in the past weeks has consisted of (1) studying the German portrayals of American society in the 1850's and 1880's, (2) studying the social scene in America during these years, (3) reading American literature of this period as it relates to European influences, (4) readings in the structure of the European family and society.

Thus my work has been interrelated, and on the whole has progressed in a unity. The specific study of German writings about America has become a part of the general study of American and European cultural trends, their differences and impacts upon one another. While shaping a Master's essay, I've gained some background in the problems of American history. I think that has been the main value of my study plan in this period.

The image of America in the eyes of the nineteenth-century German traveler is a valuable one in terms of the world today. American freedom, although darkened in one period by chattel slavery and in another by economic hardship, was seen in perspective and evaluated by the German. His judgment can help in retaining our values today.

Problems: (1) I would like to continue conferences in philosophy. The study of German writings has meaning only insofar as their German background is considered. Particularly so, since one of the main problems in this work has been the inability to establish the class and social background of each traveler and thus the reasons behind his prejudices. (2) Thus far, insufficient time to do proper readings in American history and American literature, both of which I feel are essential since I hope to continue graduate study as well as teach American history.

Of this period of study his principal teacher reported to the Committee on Graduate Studies:

Research Conference on 19th Century Immigration to the United States

Jan is doing very well. He has been carrying on research for an essay on German opinions about the United States. His problems come out of the materials. Thus far he has encountered significant reactions to religion, education, the press, and politics in America.

To accomplish his aim within the time limit, as well as to achieve other objectives perhaps even more important, we used the following procedure:

He compiled a bibliography of the writings of German travelers, immigrants, and observers from the catalogue of the New York Public Library.

We went over the titles together. Chronological periods established themselves in terms of the availability of materials. We selected 13 titles for two periods, 1850-1860 and 1880-1890.

He has already read seven volumes. For the last two conferences we went over his notes and discussed the specific issues raised by the data.

The purpose of this is twofold. In addition to the problems raised by the materials themselves, we are using the issues to begin a general reading program in American history.

He has met with nativism and has done some reading on this subject. He has now encountered a gap in the field of political institutions immediately preceding the Civil War. He is reading the following books: Alice Tyler, *Freedom's Ferment;* Arthur A. Ekirck, *Development of the Idea of Progress in the United States to 1950;* and Moisei Ostrogorski, *Democracy and the Organization of Political Parties.*

Jan also prepared a brief statement of his earlier investigation of Czech materials.

Jan's reading list to the Christmas recess follows:

For general background material in American history, sections of Merle Curti, *The Growth of American Thought,* and Alice Tyler, *Freedom's Ferment.* Both works are very helpful for gaining a picture of main trends in nineteenth-century American society.

In the more specific field of American immigration: Theodore C. Blegen, *Norwegian Migration to America;* Marcus Lee Hansen, *The Atlantic Migration;* and sections of Edith Abbott, *Historical Aspects of the Immigration Problem.* Each of the three is a different kind of model in approaching the field.

Monographs read in the field of German immigration are: Preston Albert Barba, *Emigration to America as Reflected in German Fiction;* Anna S. Levi, *Views Regarding the Adjust-*

ment of the Germans in the United States as Revealed by the German-American Press; and William Frederick Kamman, *Socialism in German-American Literature.*

Primary works, that is, writings by Germans on America ranging from the 1840's to the 1890's, read in connection with the projected Master's essay: Johann Gottfried Büttner, *Briefe aus und über Nordamerika* (1845); Franz von Löher, *Geschichte und Zustände der Deutschen in Amerika* (1847), *Amerika, Wie es Ist* (1854); Eduard Joerg, *Briefe aus den Vereinigten Staaten* (1853); Gottfried Menzel, *Die Vereinigten Staaten* (1853); Heinrich Steiner, *Künstlerfahrten vom Atlantischen bis zum Stillen Ocean* (1883); sections of Anthony Eickhoff, *In der neuen Heimath* (1884); Karl Knortz, *Amerikanische Lebensbilder* (1884); sections of Armin Tenner, ed., *Amerika. Der heutige Standpunkt der Kultur in den Vereinigten Staaten* (1884); August Sartorius von Waltershausen, *Die Zukunft des Deutschtums in den Vereinigten Staaten* (1885); Ernst Hohenwart, *Land und Leute in den Vereinigten Staaten* (1886); Jakob Mueller, *Aus den Erinnerungen eines Achundvierzigers* (1896).

Beginning a study of American literature as it related to European thought, I've read the first few chapters of *The Education of Henry Adams;* Henry James, *The American;* Herman Melville, "The Piazza" and "Benito Cereno;" and a number of letters and short stories by Mark Twain.

For a German background to emigration I've read parts of *Autorität und Familie, Studien aus den Institute für Sozialforschung;* and Erich Fromm, *Escape from Freedom.*

On February 8, Jan's principal teacher reported to the Committee on Graduate Studies:

Research Conference on 19th Century Immigration to the United States

Jan is now engaged in writing his essay. He has divided his material into specific parts and we have adopted the following procedure: He submits material to me as soon as it is completed; I then go over it carefully, noting corrections, criticisms, and comments in the margin; then discuss it during our conference. Thus far, he has done three sections and is now engaged on the fourth. I have urged him to make out a precise time schedule so as to insure the completion of the essay on time. He is working hard and making very good progress.

On March 14, his teachers sent reports to the student:

Research Conference on 19th Century Immigration to the United States

You are doing very well indeed. I am particularly pleased with the way in which you have been writing up the sections of your essay. Each effort is an improvement over the last. I think it is certain that your completed job will be a splendid one. However, I cannot impress upon you too strongly the necessity for making a time schedule and sticking to it closely. Otherwise we may find that the essay will not be done on time. We may also find that little if any opportunity remains for further reading in related fields.

American Literature Conference

Mr. Tesek has made excellent use of his reading in American Literature to supplement and round out his knowledge in this field. His search for fiction treating German immigrants in the United States was thorough, revealing that few writers have thought of Germans in America as "special" subject matter. Mr. Tesek is a thoughtful and critical reader; conference discussion shows that he has keen perceptions in relating individual reactions described in novels, autobiography, and biography to various historical currents.

On May 23, Jan Tesek submitted his Master's thesis, "The German Immigrant and his Image of the United States, 1848-54, 1880-86." The final report from his principal teacher to the Committee on Graduate Studies states:

Research Conference on 19th Century Immigration to the United States

Mr. Tesek's year was full of fine accomplishments. His essay on "The German Immigrant and his Image of the United States, 1848-54, 1880-86" gave him experience in a number of areas of social science. He learned a great deal about the technique of research in original sources. In addition, he improved his facility in the German language, since the bulk of the materials he used was written in that language. A number of important passages had to be translated for use in the essay. These were very well done. In general, the paper turned out very well indeed.

I think Mr. Tesek is a very good graduate student. He is industrious, deeply interested in history, and will do fine work wherever he goes.

Jan is now in his first teaching position in a large eastern university and is completing his doctoral thesis. Recent reports from him and from the university faculty where he studied are enthusiastic about his progress. He passed his general examination for the Ph.D. in the fall of 1954. His field of study has continued to be American history with a political emphasis; modern Britain, modern Europe with emphasis on Germany, and American literature. He has not had much time to pursue the work in immigration but many of his ideas for his dissertation stem from his Master's essay.

Apparently he found it valuable that he studied for his Master's degree in a small college, for he wrote that Master's candidates at the university must make a choice between undergraduate courses and the Ph.D. seminars.

For this student the tutorial program made it possible for him to use his first experimental graduate year quite fully in his later study.

Preparing for secondary school teaching
in a new field after raising a family

MRS. WINSTON, with a very different educational background and objective, also did her major work in American history. After completing two years of college in 1933, she married and did not return to finish her undergraduate work until her daughter entered the Sarah Lawrence Nursery School. Mrs. Winston received her A.B. degree in 1941. The major concentration of her study as an undergraduate was in psychology and early childhood education, and during her senior year she completed five hundred hours of practice teaching. Subsequent to her graduation she was a teaching associate for one year at the Sarah Lawrence Nursery School, where her teaching was highly commended. She was accepted as a candidate for the Master's degree program in September 1953.

Mrs. Winston's application for graduate study developed from her desire to prepare herself for public school teaching in another state to which she and her family, now comprising a husband and four children, planned to move after she received her Master's degree. At this time her youngest child was entering the College nursery school. Although qualified to teach nursery school, Mrs. Winston's interests had changed and she was eager to teach history on the high school level. As an undergraduate she had taken few social science courses (except in psychology) and she was aware that concentrated work in history would be demanding. But with the sympathetic help and active participation of her husband, mother-in-law, and children she believed that she could carry competently a full-time graduate program. During the years when she had been raising her family, she had read considerably and was well oriented to current social and political issues. She had participated actively and held office in the P.T.A. and the guidance committee of her local public school, the community council, and the Sarah Lawrence Alumnae Association. In interviewing her, the Committee on Graduate Studies was impressed by her warmth and understanding of children, the clarity of her thinking, and the soundness of her planning.

During her first semester she attended a course in *American Life and Thought,* and a seminar, *Ideas in America,* having weekly conferences with the teacher; she also attended a course in *The History of Europe from 1610-1815* and had regular conferences for this too. At a meeting of her faculty and her adviser on the Committee on Graduate Studies in mid-November, they agreed that Mrs. Winston was working to full capacity, had enormously increased her familiarity with historical material, and had in every way made a splendid adjustment. Her faculty recommended that her certification for a teaching post be inquired into to make certain of any specific additional requirements in the state where she planned to teach. The Committee on Graduate Studies in discussing Mrs. Winston's progress after the first semester noted that her psychological understanding of adolescents was excellent, and her major need was historical content and formulation of content. She needed background ranging over the whole scope of American history, and thus a tutorial course, in which she could discuss her reading and formulate her thinking on ways of presenting the material for high school students, seemed the right solution.

In conferring on February 10 with the superintendent of schools in the community in which she would be living, Mrs. Winston learned that although there was no immediate vacancy for a high school history teacher, there were openings in the rural one-room elementary schools in which grades five through eight were taught by one teacher. She was ready to take on and explore the teaching possibilities in such a school and considered the opportunity of teaching social studies as good preparation for later high school teaching. It was thought advisable that she attend two seminars on *Teaching Methods* and *Philosophy of Education* and spend two mornings weekly in the local school observing teaching. As the recommended work in education would be time consuming, the Committee on Graduate Studies considered how her program in the second semester could be adjusted. At this point it consisted of:

1. *American Life and Thought*
2. *Conference Studies in American History,*
related to secondary school teaching
3. *The History of Europe from 1610-1815*

Although Mrs. Winston recognized the need for reducing her academic load, she wished to continue her work in *The History of Europe from 1610-1815* which paralleled that in *American Life and Thought*. In the latter course, therefore, the original plan for an extended written study on "The Origin of the Bill of Rights" was abandoned in favor of the conference course named above. Mrs. Winston at this time became an auditor in *The History of Europe,* thus freeing a substantial portion of her time for work in the education seminars.

On May 28, her faculty reported:

Conference Studies in American History

Mrs. Winston's conference course with me has been in the general development of United States history. Taking as a base of departure her course in *American Life and Thought,* we have dug in at different points of history, discussing and reading in more detailed fashion such areas as the clashes over the Constitution, the nature of civil liberties, Jeffersonian and Jacksonian democracy, the Civil War, the corporate revolution, the philosophy of W. G. Sumner, William James, and so forth. Mrs. Winston has handled these competently and with commendable critical ability. She is also developing an awareness of the bibliography of American social science which should be of help to her as a student and a teacher.

The History of Europe from 1610-1815

Mrs. Winston has spent this last term as an auditor. She has, however, continued to do a substantial amount of the reading assigned, and has participated in class discussions. Her participation in the course has familiarized her and put her in touch with this area of historical study.

Seminar: History and Philosophy of American Education
Methods in Education
Problems in American Schools

Mrs. Winston did satisfactory work with me during the spring term. Her discussions were helpful and her ability to interpret problems of education offered a stimulating experience for other members of the class.

Mrs. Winston's graduate program required both extensive and intensive reading in a field for which she had had limited undergraduate preparation. Through the revised plan for work related to American history, she received specific help in formulating historical materials for high school teaching. Seminars in education were added primarily so that she might qualify for teaching in the upper elementary grades. She felt that these seminars and her observations of teaching were as valuable for secondary as for elementary education. Mrs. Winston was fortunate in that she had fulfilled the practice teaching requirement prior to her graduate study; it was this which made it possible for her to study in a major subject field and qualify for teaching in one year.

In the summer of 1954, Mrs. Winston and her family moved to their new home, and in September she began teaching in a rural elementary school. She was well pleased with her graduate year and anticipated a vigorous teaching experience. The Committee on Graduate Studies was equally pleased with the use she was able to make of a concentrated year of work in the fields of history and education, and believes that young people will profit by Mrs. Winston's broad vision and understanding of the background and development of crucial social and political issues.

Training in a special field after
a broad undergraduate program

Mrs. DuBois entered Sarah Lawrence College as a junior transfer and received the A.B. degree in May 1952. Her interest was focused particularly in literature, in which she was an outstanding student. As an undergraduate at Sarah Lawrence she had taken *American Literature, The Comic Spirit in Literature, Folklore and Myth,* and *Russian Literature.* In related areas, she had studied in *The Individual and History,* which makes an historical approach to problems in philosophy and social philosophy; and a seminar course, *Ideas in America,* where she was able to do extended work in a combination of historical and literary studies.

When Mrs. Dubois became interested in secondary school and college teaching of literature and applied to our Graduate Studies Program, we were pleased to accept her, in September 1952, both because she was an able student and because we felt that our program would prepare her well for teaching. Her M.A. program took into consideration the possibility of future work toward the Ph.D., which she hoped to obtain. She had studied Latin for two years but did not have a reading knowledge of French and German. The Committee on Graduate Studies advised that she study French, preferably beginning in the summer of 1952. The French was considered to be outside the Master of Arts program, as graduate credit is not given for beginning work in a language. The study of German was to be deferred.

Mrs. Dubois had been well prepared in specialized areas of literature. She needed to extend the range of her knowledge of English literature. The following program was approved by the Committee on Graduate Studies:

1. *Renaissance Literature:* She attended this class and had conference work with the teacher as the major portion of her work. She needed intensive reading in the literature of the Renaissance.

    2. *Conference Studies in 18th and 19th Century Literature,* working with several members of the Literature faculty.

    3. *Beginning French* (non-credit)

Her December 15 faculty reports give a picture of the work she had covered during the first third of the year:

Renaissance Literature

Mrs. Dubois has done all of the work for my course in Renaissance Literature in a very satisfactory fashion. She is intelligent, enthusiastic about literature, and very industrious. In addition, we have worked in conference on some of Shakespeare's tragedies and chronicle plays, literary criticism, and English history. I have found her very responsive and most rewarding to work with.

Conference Studies in 18th and 19th Century Literature

Mrs. Dubois is an excellent reader, quick to understand the reading in hand and to ask questions when she thinks she may have misunderstood. At first she was over-zealous in trying to discover connections between the Restoration and the Renaissance; consequently she did this on a superficial level. As our work together went on, she seemed to me to understand that becoming acquainted with English Literature in its historical development was not a process of adding *this to that,* but one of assimilating and organizing materials in terms meaningful to herself. She has real intellectual curiosity, and I feel sure that she will gain momentum and make an excellent showing after working with several members of the Literature faculty in periods in which she has read very little. Quality of reading is excellent.

Beginning French

Mrs. Dubois worked with energy and understanding. She has obtained excellent results. She takes active part in class discussions and her work is distinctly superior to that of the other students. She audits the *Intermediate French* course once a week and understands French to the extent that the course becomes useful for her. She has profitably read a literary French text of a certain difficulty. Her final test was excellent.

On March 13 Mrs. Dubois replied as follows to the Committee on Graduate Studies' inquiry: What are the main values in your study plan and in your work generally?

My original intention in planning my program of graduate studies was to become more familiar with the historical development of English Literature. I felt that there were certain periods in which I had read very little, and that I lacked a sense of historical and literary continuity. My assumption was that in a work of art there is, in addition to that which is original, new and personal, a tradition which operates very subtly through the creativity of the artist. This force is historical, dynamic, and with a few exceptions apparent in the works of the English writers. It seemed to me that the only way to get in touch with this cultural "gestalt" in literature was to read as widely as possible.

I feel, then, that my program has been extremely successful. If I had been forced to concentrate on a thesis subject, my actual reading time would have been cut in half, and my knowledge of literature would have continued to be spotty. Since I have been reading in several periods of English literature, I have worked with members of the Literature faculty with whom I might otherwise have had no contact. This has, of course, been a pleasure.

My study of French has been extremely valuable and has already been of use to me—e.g., I have finally been able to read the conversations between Claudia Chauchat and Hans Castorp, and between Henry V and Katherine. By auditing the *Intermediate French* class, I have been able to follow some of the class discussions on French literature. Since there are many cross-currents between France and England (particularly in the 17th and 18th Centuries), I found it extremely worth while to study French this year along with my regular graduate work in literature.

I also feel that it has been a good plan to carry one literature course steadily throughout the year. My *Renaissance Literature* course has been an excellent anchor for the rest of my work.

Since I have a regular weekly conference with the teacher, I am able to discuss the general direction of my readings in literature with him. I am very happy, too, that the Committee on Graduate Studies approved of my auditing classes in *Intermediate French* and *Shakespeare*.

My graduate work at Sarah Lawrence has been very satisfying for other reasons—greater freedom of thought and expression, closer work with the professors, no need for repetition of subjects already completed as an undergraduate, more time for assembling and assimilating knowledge. Best of all—the chance to work seriously in an atmosphere which is free from pedantry.

This student's work report on her studies during the second term (January to mid-March) is given in full:

1. *Renaissance Literature*
   A. Class assignments completed:

Christopher Marlowe	*Dr. Faustus*
Ben Johnson	*Every Man in his Humor*
	The Alchemist
	The Poetaster (with oral report to class on the "War of the Theaters")
Thomas Kyd	*The Spanish Tragedy*
John Webster	*The Duchess of Malfi*
J. Fletcher and F. Beaumont	*The Knight of the Burning Pestle*
Izaak Walton	*The Compleat Angler*
Sir Thomas Malory	*Le Morte D'Arthur*, Selected readings
John Milton	*Of Education*
	Areopagitica
	Minor Poems (sonnets, "Lycidas," "L'Allegro," etc.)
	Comus
	Paradise Lost (completed up to Book VII)
Michel Montaigne	*Essays*, Selected readings

64

B. Conference reading completed:

William Shakespeare	*The Merchant of Venice*
	Twelfth Night
	A Midsummer Night's Dream
	Henry IV, Part II
	Julius Caesar
Geoffrey Chaucer	*The Canterbury Tales:*
	Prioress, Prologue and Tale
	Pardoner, Prologue and Tale
	Miller, Prologue and Tale
	Knight, Prologue and Tale

C. For conference work this semester in *Renaissance Literature* I have continued to follow the class assignments in the *Shakespeare* course. However, since I felt that I was learning enough about Shakespeare by auditing this course, I began a study of Chaucer in my hour conference for *Renaissance Literature*. Possibly the most important aspect of my conference work this semester is that I finally learned to read Chaucer aloud in Middle English. Mr. M. succeeded in convincing me that my previously inept translations of *The Canterbury Tales* were unsatisfactory and that Nevill Coghill could never take the place of Chaucer himself. After many painful sessions with Mr. M.'s tape recorder, I can now read aloud with some ease, and my silent reading of Chaucer has improved greatly. I found all the class reading assignments extremely interesting, and when I read the work for a second time *(Paradise Lost)*, I felt that I gained a deeper understanding.

2. *Conference Studies in 18th and 19th Century Literature*
   A. Conference reading completed:

Henry Fielding	*Joseph Andrews, Tom Jones*
Tobias Smollet	*Roderick Random*
Laurence Sterne	*Tristram Shandy*
"Monk" Lewis	*Vathek*
Frances Burney	*Evelina*
William Godwin	*Caleb Williams*
Ernest A. Baker	*The History of the English Novel*
	Volume IV (for reference)

B. Reading *Tom Jones* was an experience which I would hate to have missed. Fielding is delightful in every way. Mr. K. was a great help in pointing out the historical interest of each novel, as well as the possible contemporary applications.

3. *Beginning French*
   A. Class reading completed:
      Jean Anouilh   *Antigone*

Inasmuch as Mrs. Dubois needed long-range study in several periods of English literature and her ability to write a first-rate critical essay had been amply demonstrated as an undergraduate, it had been agreed by her faculty and the Committee on Graduate Studies that she would take an oral examination in completion of her work for the M.A. degree. Her principal teacher made these comments on the oral examination:

The Committee for the oral consisted of the Dean and five members of the Literature faculty. It was scheduled to take about half an hour, but went so well that it went on for about an hour and twenty minutes.

We started with a question about Sidney as a literary critic. She answered well, first about the general theory involved in his essay on poetry and later, when pressed, the specific references. This led to Spenser and eventually to Elizabethan drama (and Dryden as a critic of) and to Shakespeare. The questioning here was quite searching and demanded all her resources. This part she handled fairly well, if without distinction.

Questioning then moved to Chaucer (versatile and civilized exemplar of age, etc.). We were at no point concerned to quiz her on specific items, but to use what she had read for the purpose of critical discussion. Chaucer led into the general field of satire. Some time was spent on the nature of satire, its general principles. Applications led us all the way to Byron.

There was also some discussion of Romantic poetry. On the basis of her remarks on poetical effects in Keats, she was questioned closely and pressed into specific definitions. Her responses showed a good mind and a sensitive ear.

There was material on the novel, one of her best fields.

We were not after information; we wanted to see how meaningful her fair knowledge of English literature was for her.

Our conclusion was that she had shown ability with which we could feel pleased. She was at ease and enjoyed the oral in process. So did the examiners.

Combining dance with the liberal arts after a specialized professional background

JOAN BRENT, one of six M.A. candidates in dance, presents a fairly typical picture of the graduate dance students. In her application to Sarah Lawrence College she wrote that while attending college she had spent five summers in studying dance under Martha Graham, Hanya Holm, and Louis Horst, and after her graduation had toured France and England as a member of a professional dance company. Whether because the life of a professional dancer is a precarious one, or because of a genuine interest in teaching, or because she felt her talents to lie in teaching rather than on the dance concert stage, she decided to prepare to teach dance in a college. The opportunity to teach and study dance in colleges is much greater than it was ten years ago, and many institutions are discovering the importance in both aesthetic and physical values, of having a dance program in the curriculum.

Joan's registration adviser at Sarah Lawrence in September 1950 commented that "she is alert, intelligent and eager to work. Her academic background is rather sketchy. A professional dancer, she has concentrated so much on dance and related fields that time for general education was limited. She realizes the gaps in her education and wants to fill them in." The following program was recommended by her adviser and approved by the Committee on Graduate Studies:

1. *Program in Dance*
2. *Studies in Modern Poetry*
3. *Culture and Personality* (including readings in sociology and psychology)
4. *The Artist in Modern Society* (literature, audit)

The Committee on Graduate Studies and her faculty agreed that at least half of her work would be in anthropology and literature, that her work in dance would be focused toward preparation for teaching dance.

Her learning problems and progress throughout her year's work are clearly reflected in the periodic evaluations of her faculty and her analysis of her learning experiences, as revealed in their reports:

Program in Dance   October 31, 1950

Joan has been a very interesting student to work with. She is spending about one-half of her time in dance and is making very good use of the time. She wants to teach dance in a college and her work with us (not only in dance) is slanted toward this aim. She has become a member of several classes (*Technique* and *Composition*) which she observes during participation. She is doing some choreography and directing, and is directed in turn by other students. She has read mainly about the teaching of dance and her discussions are concerned with that.

Participation and observation make her constantly more aware of teaching problems which interest her keenly and to which she is very seriously trying to find her own answers.

Eventually she will observe dance as taught at colleges in New York and environs, and teach a short series of classes here at the College.

Studies in Modern Poetry   October 31, 1950

She has moved in a very interesting way over the last month. Mainly she has been troubled with words, with the necessity of talking about something she is perfectly aware of intuitively. Everything is having great consequences for her; she is all the time busy with it.

In a sense, she is less prepared for *Poetry* than others in the class—her background is sketchy, her judgments (when she makes them) are tentative and uncertain. On the other hand, she is extremely responsive; one can see the work making a difference in her. It will be some time before her reading makes a clear pattern. I think this must not be hurried, but allowed to settle, because she is thinking her work through, very slowly and very carefully. At present, the greatest danger is that of overburdening her mind with too much material. She has done her class work very carefully and thoroughly and always has a crop of consequent points to question me on.

In view of all this, I was not too ready to begin extra work with her. Inevitably, however, we began to discuss the relation between poetry and dance, for she cannot help considering everything in relation to dance at some point. So I have devoted extra conference time with her to discussion along those lines, and intend to let this develop itself through the year. Out of the additional reading she is doing in this direction and the discussion, she will assemble enough material for a fairly conclusive paper, or whatever else we decide would be best.

She does not join very much in class discussion, but all her conference work has been very eager and full. I think she is working extremely hard in *Poetry*. She is perpetually aware of two things—one, how little time there is; two, how complex words are.

Culture and Personality   October 31, 1950

Her first concrete assignment for conference was to analyze Zuñi mythology and draw from the class comments as to the fundamental attitudes and values in Zuñi culture. She did this very well, with reasonable thoroughness and with good imagination. While her conference work reflects a weak background in social science, she has impressed me with a quickness to learn, with strong curiosity, and a good deal of diligence. She has contributed intelligently to class discussion. I am not encouraging her to relate anthropology too closely to dance at this time. At the moment I feel pretty optimistic about her work in anthropology.

Program in Dance   February 7, 1951

The past month has served to acquaint Joan with some of the by-products of dance teaching. Occasioned by the appearance of our dance students at Carnegie Hall, she was given some responsibility about buying materials, designing and sewing costumes. Further, she instructed the group on how to use make-up and supervised that part of the performance. Joan does these things in workmanlike fashion but rather without initiative or much imagination or interest. Perhaps she needs to feel fully in charge of the situation to take firmer hold; this opportunity she will have since her major project is to be fully directed and costumed by her.

Studies in Modern Poetry   February 7, 1951

The last month has uncovered, in her work on Yeats, her lack of a wide frame of reference, her ignorance of fairly fundamental philosophical concepts.

She works from the poet up, has to invent her own terms. Although she wrote a good paper, I felt that this required a great deal of labor on her part. The lack of order in her mind shows in the lack of order in her work.

She still asks good questions, responds quickly to what she reads. I do not want to suggest that we should make her into a philosopher. Apart from the difficulty of that, I think it important to preserve her spontaneous response to poetry. The task still is really one of helping her to control and order it, within her capabilities.

Culture and Personality   February 7, 1951

She has been going along pretty much as before, and there is little new to report. She herself has the feeling that she is understanding a good deal more of the course than before. This is true. We have discussed the level of her work in the course and I am satisfied that she learn the more general and also useful concepts of the course. This she is doing.

"Yes," she said in her own report (March 1, 1951), "this program does seem adequate." And continued:

I do find it rather difficult to keep the proposed division of time to be spent on my courses constant, as I work best when I concentrate my energies more towards one goal. But I think in general terms the balance remains as expected.

My anthropology teacher seems newly aware of my needs, which lie in dealing with larger questions rather than specific details. My next study is to be of the Incas, particularly the emotional tone of their religion, and how it ties in with the present day South American culture.

The *Dance* and *Modern Poetry* courses are going well. The fact that my proposed graduate project will probably involve

70

material discussed in the *Poetry* conference periods will make it possible to bring a good deal of the year's work to a sharp focus. In addition to the regular conference work we are doing in regard to dance, I have been assigned other poets to read for a general background.

Joan's work reports for this period, given below, add substance to her general comments:

1. *Program in Dance*
   Attended music listening classes
   Attended acting classes
   Took part in Carnegie Hall concert
   Performed solo at Hunter under Theatre Dance, Inc., the music for which was written by Edmund Haines

   CONFERENCE WORK:
   Discussion of problem involved in music composition and costuming for dance
   Field trip to buy materials for Carnegie costumes
   Further discussion on dance criticism

2. *Studies in Modern Poetry*

   BIBLIOGRAPHY (since December 1):

Karl Shapiro	*Essay on Rime*, Sec. 3 "The Confusion of Belief"
Robert Frost	*Collected Poems*
	Essay "The figure a poem makes"
Mark Schorer	*Criticism*
Stephen Spender	Essay "The making of a poem"
William Saroyan	*To Write a Poem*
William Butler Yeats	*Collected Poems*
Donald Stauffer	*The Golden Nightingale*, Chapter II, "Speech on the situation of the poet Emmanuel"
Cleanth Brooks	*The Well Wrought Urn*, Essay "Yeats Great Rooted Blossomer"
Robinson Jeffers	*Selected Poems*
Oscar Williams	*Little Treasury of Modern Poetry*, Selections

71

Gertrude Stein	*Selected Writing,* Selections from *Tender Buttons*
Christopher Fry	"A Playwright Speaks"
Dylan Thomas	*Selected Writings*
Francis Scarfe	*Auden and After* "The Liberation of Poetry"
Hart Crane	*Collected Poems of Hart Crane*
Brom Weber	*Hart Crane*

CONFERENCE WORK:

Selected writings of William Carlos Williams, D. H. Lawrence, A. E. Housman, Genevieve Taggard
Composed two dances to poems
Wrote two original poems

PAPERS:

1. On Yeats "Words for Music, Perhaps"
2. On Two Poems of Dylan Thomas

3. *Culture and Personality*

BIBLIOGRAPHY (since December 1):

Selections from:

Geza Roheim	*Psychoanalysis and Anthropology*
Patrick Mullahy	*Oedipus—Myth and Complex*
Erich Fromm	*Escape from Freedom*
Irving Goldman	"The Psychiatric Interpretation of Russian History"
Clyde Kluckhohn	*Mirror for Man*
Henry A. Murray	*Personality,* Chapters by Gillin, Erickson, Hallowell & Eggan
Douglas G. Haring	*Personal Character and Cultural Milieu*
Margaret Mead	"Age Patterning in Personality"
Clyde Kluckhohn	"Some Aspects of Navaho Infancy and Early Childhood"

Material in:

Cora A. Dubois	*People of Alor*
Irving Goldman	"The Ifugao" in *Cooperation and Competition among Primitive People*

72

R. F. Barton *Half-way Sun*
Philippine Pagans

CONFERENCE WORK:

Discussion of Abram Kardiner's analysis of the Alorese in *The Individual and His Society*

Discussion of cross-culture comparison of Alor, Tanata, Betsileo, Ifugao

Read and discussed R. H. Tawney, *Religion and the Rise of Capitalism*

READ:

Paul Radin, *Primitive Religion*

R. H. Lowie, *Primitive Religion*

In early March, the Committee reviewed Joan's experience and planned the culmination of her year on the basis of a recommendation from her principal teacher:

Tentative plan for Joan Brent's major project   March 7, 1951

Since dance is her major interest, her project is to be a "summing up" of some of the experiments she has made in this field.

Teaching of dance at college level has been the subject of most of her weekly conferences. Up to now that has been primarily theoretical, but for the next three weeks, Joan will be teaching two periods weekly on movement techniques in the regular dance program. This is to give her an opportunity to do practice teaching of beginning as well as advanced students. Her lesson plans have been worked out in conference. I shall be present when she is teaching and shall discuss her teaching with her each week and finally will report my observations to the Committee.

Her teaching, however, will be only a preliminary part of her project. The plan is to let Joan have approximately one-third of the program of the proposed Dance evening on May 16 for a showing of her own choreography.

Joan has brought to her work in poetry much interest and many questions about the problems of the use of spoken words as an accompaniment or as an intrinsic part of dance composition. This has led to much discussion and search for usable material and is finally producing several experiments. Mr. A. has

73

suggested that Joan bring all her findings, pro and con, on to paper in an outline form which will contain suggestions and warnings useful to other students who are interested in the problems of dance and words.

Joan will perform dance studies which have resulted from this work. Her experiments are to include studies using poems by Mr. A. and by Joan herself as well as an adaptation of the work of a poet she has chosen.

Further, her part in the May program will contain a solo dance composed earlier in the year and based freely on legendary material of the Zuñi Indian. The impetus of this dance came out of her work in anthropology. Finally, she is working on a dance (a solo and duet) in the style of the Baroque period.

This scheme seems to touch on all the areas Joan has been most concerned with during the year. Since it did not seem possible to make these experiences come out on paper, or in one dance, this seems the very best way of presenting the total design of her work. Certainly it should reveal the calibre of her thinking and allow us to see something of her ability as a teacher, since all dances will have to be her own choreography and when not performed by herself will be the product of her teaching and directing.

Designing of costumes, staging and lighting will also be expected of her.

On May 25, Joan's faculty sent in their evaluations of her achievement throughout the year.

Program in Dance   May 25, 1951

The important points to say in summary are perhaps that: (a) Joan has become a student who has found deep satisfaction in learning and thinking and who will unquestionably continue to widen and deepen the scope of what she knows; (b) that she accomplished what she set out to do—to learn about teaching Dance at college level; and (c) that she set a standard of work in her major field that will require lively effort to maintain.

Studies in Modern Poetry

A review of Joan's work over the year must point up especially her very remarkable transition from a bewildered newcomer, with very little breadth of knowledge or conceptual experience, to a capable student, becoming surer in her judgment and increasingly sensitive to her reading. In Poetry, although she had always a natural emotional response to it, she was absorbed to the extent of being completely swamped by its impact and by the forced extension of her ideas. Her most distinguished achievement, however, has been her subsequent tenacity in making order out of the chaos of new experience. She has become a distinctly different person, newly aware of what has still to be done, and in responsible possession of her gains in experience this year.

Culture and Personality

Her final paper on the Inca Civilization represents a satisfactory analysis of the main features of a relatively complex culture. In the light of her previous lack of preparation in social science this is a considerable and very satisfying achievement.

Although Joan's intensive training in dance enabled her to make immediate use of her teacher's help in teacher preparation, her sketchy liberal arts background retarded for a number of months her ability to make comparably good use of her anthropology and poetry courses. Of great importance, however, in her subsequent functioning as a dance teacher were the intellectual insights learned and the intellectual curiosity aroused.

Three years later she writes that she is married and the mother of a six-months old son. After leaving Sarah Lawrence she spent a year as a valuable dance teacher at a university. Then, in 1952, she married and taught dance and worked with a community theatre group. Currently she is teaching modern, folk and square dancing with a community recreation department, dancing with a university group, and doing choreography on her own. She comments that "I can't think of a more valuable year to me than the one I spent at Sarah Lawrence. I am still learning from it."

*Supplementing vocational training for elementary
education with theory, literature, and music*

THE UNDERGRADUATE program of Ivy Chase represents a considerably different experience from that of most of the other students in the Master's program. A graduate of a teacher's training college, from which she had received a B.S. degree in 1951, she had previously worked in nursery school and early childhood education on a program which prepared her to teach pre-primary and early elementary grades. She was highly recommended as a teacher of young children and as a candidate for the Master's degree. The Committee on Graduate Studies, well aware of the gaps in her education, were impressed by her earnest desire to widen her intellectual horizons. She planned to continue with nursery school teaching after receiving her Master's degree.

Unlike most of our students interested in nursery school or elementary school teaching, this young woman came with a specialized technical training, overspecialized in the undergraduate years, needing the general background which would give scope and substance to her specialized training. Although in an altogether different field, she presented an educational problem not unlike that of Joan Brent who, trained as a dancer, needed a better education to make her a good dancer or teacher of dance. This student needed educational experience which would help her generalize on her experience as a teachers' college graduate and a teacher of children. Whether providing this kind of education would amount to a year of study deserving the Master's degree was a question which concerned the Committee on Graduate Studies. It was somewhat more difficult to justify this program than Joan Brent's, since the studies making up Miss Brent's year would relate so directly to her special field and her teaching.

Miss Chase's main field of study was psychology, her main work in *The Psychology of Personality.* She had taken courses in *Human Dynamics* and *Human Growth and Development,* but had no clear concept of what constituted the total personality. Although she had taken many education courses, she had never been exposed to theories of learning nor had she had experience with scientific methods.

She was interested in music, and used music in her teaching, but her training in music for children had been highly specialized, giving her no general understanding of musical form either for her own use or for use in her teaching of music. She was therefore advised to do work in *Keyboard Harmony* as a minor field.

As an undergraduate, Miss Chase had had only two courses in literature, both survey courses, and as a graduate student a second minor study was planned in the field of literature—a course in *The Comic Spirit in Literature.*

On November 28 Miss Chase's faculty met and agreed that the purposes for which she came to Sarah Lawrence were being met. No changes were indicated in her program.

On February 2 she received the following evaluations from her faculty:

Psychology of Personality

Your enthusiasm is very evident, especially in terms of your readiness to undertake a great deal of work. Your stated aim when you were applying was that you wanted a year of study to knit together the practical work you had done. You are making real progress toward this goal. This isn't an easy aim to achieve, since tying up theory and practice is an intricate job even for a person who has real talent in both areas. But it is a necessary one to attempt constantly since, as you remark in your self-evaluation, ideas about people often help us relate to them in a different and, we hope, a more insightful way.

The project you have outlined is a useful and ambitious one, but I believe you will be able to manage it. Don't forget selectivity is also a crucial part of learning, and so don't attempt to say everything at once.

One point which we have talked about in conference in terms of your "idealistic views," and in your self-evaluation in terms of "relying on many of my own personal reactions," needs to be mentioned. You have a tendency to evaluate in overly subjective terms. In itself this isn't necessarily a handicap as long as one knows what these terms are and can also see a problem in other frameworks. Use yourself as an instrument, but become clearer as to what this instrument is like. All in all, a very good start.

Keyboard Harmony

Your work for this first semester has been very good indeed. Your enthusiasm and interest have been matched by your intelligent and thorough preparation for the weekly conference. The progress you have made—both in your intellectual understanding and your physical ability to produce aurally this understanding—is particularly gratifying since this was a completely new and somewhat difficult medium for you last September. There is every reason to believe that the direction the work follows will be of real practical value to you in your future work with children. A most encouraging beginning. No suggestions to offer other than that the present high calibre of work continue for the remainder of the year.

The Comic Spirit in Literature

You have made noticeable progress in your ability to evaluate the books you read. From the first experiments in conference work with the plays of Shakespeare, you eventually evolved a technique for criticism which appears to be proving useful to you. In fact, I feel that now you are able to understand and appraise many books which would have been close to meaningless to you last fall—particularly such things as Gide's *The Counterfeiters*. Your papers have also improved, and have been decidedly more varied and fresh in their approach. Altogether, good work.

On March 13, Ivy replied to an inquiry from the Committee on Graduate Studies: What are the main values in your study plan and in your work generally?

The course in *Personality* has given me additional material in the field of psychology. I have learned different methods of approach in dealing with the same subject. My knowledge of the authors in the field of psychology—and its related areas—has grown considerably. The study of early childhood has provided me with greater understanding of young children . . . this being of utmost importance in my future work as a nursery school teacher. In each of the units that we have studied in the class in *Personality,* I have become more aware of the world about me and of the people within this universe. For me, there has developed an urgency to work for better human relationships!

The conference course in *Keyboard Harmony* has provided me with a deeper understanding of music. It has been a delightful, valuable experience.

The course in *The Comic Spirit in Literature* has provided me with experiences completely different from those in my past formal education. Not only have I become aware of the comic spirit in literature, but also I have learned to seek out the comic spirit in life. My attitude in daily living has changed considerably since my arrival at Sarah Lawrence! The class discussions prove to be more valuable each week as I am gaining a more critical approach in my reading.

It would not be fair to omit the values that I gain from my weekly conference meetings. It is at these times that I become more aware of my personal development. With the individual teacher, I am guided towards more mature thinking and to more exact interpretations. The choice of materials covered is discussed in order that I may gain a more 'wholistic' education rather than an inhibited kind of study in one particular area. I am most grateful for this.

It is indeed difficult to describe my attitude towards my study plan. There are many 'unmentionable' values that I 'feel' are additionally important in my work generally. I can freely admit that I have developed into a more independent, scientific thinker, a happier, more integrated person, and I am much better equipped intellectually for my future since I started my graduate studies at Sarah Lawrence.

The final reports of Miss Chase's teachers give their evaluation of her learning:

Psychology of Personality

Recalling her aim in applying for a year of study here, that she wanted a chance to think through and pull together previous experiences which were largely practical in nature, I realize that she has made real progress toward this goal. She has met all her work conscientiously and has caught onto the ideas fairly well, though mostly on the level of duplicating them rather than recreating them. I think she needs lots of time to make experiences into her own so that they are something she can use critically and discriminatingly. The feature that we all noted, namely her unbridled enthusiasm, shows itself in a rapid swallowing of ideas, with the critical digestive process not too much in evidence.

I say these things with her major paper uppermost in mind. I confess to some disappointment with it. The project we worked out was an ambitious one and especially when I think of what I had in mind, a difficult one for any graduate student to carry through. I pushed very hard in the direction of having her draw relations between theory of child development and nursery school practice. Yet I wished she had been more critical of her past experiences and had brought more quickly to bear the ideas we had discussed in class and conference. She writes vividly about children and has a flair for capturing a real episode on paper. She did fairly well in choosing examples of children's activities as illustrations of points she was making. However, since the discussion of these points was relatively brief and largely borrowed (many quotes) the examples made up a big part of the paper.

She worked a great deal and very hard. I believe that the effort was decidedly worth while for herself although nothing original was produced. She will be an excellent nursery school teacher, though she still needs to work out a tendency toward fixed, pre-set ways of understanding what children are about.

Keyboard Harmony

Miss Chase's work has continued to be highly satisfactory. It has been characterized by her tremendous enthusiasm, her complete receptivity, her consistently thorough and thoughtful preparation for the weekly conferences. Her keyboard facility and harmonic thinking have become much surer and quicker. It has been quite a beneficial year of study. She needs much more work in this subject for it to be truly "useful" for her, but she has made an excellent beginning.

The Comic Spirit in Literature

This student has continued to work with enthusiasm and steadiness in a thoroughly satisfactory manner. She has, I believe, come a long way this year in achieving a more mature approach to reading. She is not yet highly selective, accepting almost everything she reads with equal delight. This is partially because she is so anxious to learn more that she assumes anything presented for reading by a teacher is too good and too important to reject. On the other hand it displays a catholicity of interests which should be useful to her in teaching.

On paper this program seems perhaps the most questionable for a Master's degree of the group here described; and the student herself, as the final report from the psychology professor indicates, was not very well equipped, temperamentally or intellectually, or by previous training, for the kind of theoretical study outlined for her. However, her general needs seemed great enough to warrant allowing a more diverse program than that followed by most students, at the same time demanding theoretical studies related to her own field. There is no doubt that she had the ability to be an excellent nursery school teacher; and in fulfilling the goals of providing her with a broader knowledge of literature and music, and at the same time with the psychological foundations for her previous knowledge of children, this program was valid.

Studying American culture as background for
teaching American literature in European schools

KAREN ROSENCRANTZ, a student from a Danish university, applied for admission to the Master of Arts program in order to prepare herself for teaching American literature in her native folk schools and to gather materials for her Doctoral dissertation at the university. While at the university she had received scholarships for summer study in France, Germany, and Norway. She had worked to pay for most of her education, in jobs ranging from charwoman to teacher and including housemaid, gardener, laboratory technician, and clerk. She had been employed both as substitute and permanent teacher in Denmark, with English and physical education as major subjects.

Her interest in teaching American literature developed from three university seminars in literature she had attended in Denmark, taught by American professors. As this interest grew, she became increasingly aware of her lack of understanding of the United States and sought advice from her professors. Since she had disliked large classes and lectures and wanted to study in a small college in the United States, Sarah Lawrence was suggested to her and her sponsors recommended her to Sarah Lawrence for graduate study as a mature, self-reliant, superior student.

Karen had read many American novels and plays, and some poetry but felt that she had no social or cultural context for her knowledge. She knew little of the early intellectual history of the United States. Her registration adviser at Sarah Lawrence, a teacher of American literature, wrote to the Committee, "What this student wants most is a background in American history, as her studies were in the field of literature for two full academic years. Because she will be teaching American literature, a foreign literature in Denmark, the opportunity of knowing how European literature is presented to American students appealed to her. She has already read a good deal of the literature studied in our *Modern European Literature* and will probably be able to participate in class discussions. Her real enthusiasm in American literature is in the contemporary field. I think it would be useful for her to read more Faulkner and to become acquainted with other modern novelists."

Karen's program for the first semester consisted of:

1. Working with her principal teacher in
   a. *American Life and Thought*
   b. *Seminar: Ideas in America*
2. *20th Century European Literature*
   After her first semester she was to change to
      Conference Work in American Literature

To find herself with a principal teacher and two-thirds of her work in an unfamiliar field was initially difficult for Karen. Her knowledge of the English language was good, but the vocabulary of history and politics was strange to her. After a few weeks of hard work she developed confidence in her ability and began to feel more comfortable. By mid-November she was doing good work on an advanced level which was getting steadily better. From the outset her work in European literature revealed that she knew what she was doing and where she was going. Her faculty agreed that she was a very good student, surmounting her difficulties and making progress. It was decided that she should write an essay comparing American and Danish political institutions and continue with European literature until February, when she would begin conference work in American literature.

Her work in *American Life and Thought* consisted of attending a class for an hour and a half a week, one hour conference weekly, and readings which included: R. A. Billington, B. J. Loewenberg, and S. H. Brockunier, *The United States;* Curtis P. Nettels, *Roots of American Civilization;* Charles and Mary Beard, *The Rise of American Civilization;* John Dewey, *The Public and its Problems;* E. E. Schattschneider, *The Party System;* Carl Becker, *The Beginning of the American People;* Max Farrand, *Framing the Constitution;* and a substantial number of other works.

On February 2, 1954 her faculty evaluated her work:

Seminar: Ideas in America
American Life and Thought

Miss Rosencrantz has done very good work. She has made considerable progress in overcoming her initial difficulties. She has not only advanced in her comprehension of the language, but she has been able to absorb a great deal about America. Her specific work has latterly been more than simply good, and her immediate plans for the rest of the year promise even more. The only note of caution that I think should be introduced at this point is this: she should not get wound up in her project on comparative political institutions. This was designed as an exercise, not a treatise.

20th Century European Literature

Good, mature work, excellent capacity for relating facts and ideas, solid background in history and literature. Should pay more attention to the purely formal, aesthetic aspects of novels she studies.

Karen wished to continue to audit *20th Century European Literature* after beginning her work in American literature, as she was familiar with many of the books being discussed and felt she gained much from the way the class was conducted and from class discussions. She was interested in the thinking and reactions of American students to European literature. She was frequently conscious of lacks in their background knowledge and felt that they were in the same situation that she had known when studying American literature in Europe.

The *Seminar: Ideas in America* terminated February 1, and for the following six weeks Karen worked on her essay, comparing the Danish Parliament and the American Congress.

On March 15 she wrote to the Committee on Graduate Studies in answer to the question: What are the main values in your study plan and in your work generally?

It is very difficult for me to extract the main values in my studies and work from the experience of living here as a whole. I would rather put it this way, that the work I have done, especially in American history, has added a new dimension to what I see and learn from day to day. It has cleared up a lot of riddles in the notions I had about the United States before I arrived, it has changed my attitude and comprehension of many current events by placing them in a context of which I had been ignorant. It has made it possible for me to follow and partake in discussions at the Intercollegiate Conference and on the T.V.A. trip with some kind of understanding; last but not least it has given to me the pleasure of being able to read a newspaper and look at T.V.A. with a feeling that I know what is going on.

The courses taken in literature did not bring that much of a transformation, but have proved valuable by giving me other perspectives in the teaching of literature, and giving me the opportunity of listening to the interpretations of my teachers and fellow students.

After spring vacation, during which she had visited T.V.A., Washington, and several Southern colleges and universities with a group of Sarah Lawrence students, Miss Rosencrantz was invited to speak on Elementary and Secondary Education in Denmark at a seminar in education, and became so interested in the discussion by American students on educational problems that she continued to attend the seminar.

Her May 28 faculty reports follow:

84

Backgrounds of American Literature

Attended and participated in class discussions on Mark Twain, Henry James (twice), William Dean Howells, Hamlin Garland, Sarah Orne Jewett, Stephen Crane.

Read, for conference, *The Ambassadors,* and wrote a critical paper.

Also for conference, several novels and short stories by Willa Cather. Paper on the pattern of society as reflected in her Mid-Western stories.

Her class and conference discussion good. She showed strength in establishing relationships with other literature and with her observations of life in the United States.

Her papers reflected the pressure on her time. Except for its too abrupt conclusion, the James paper was excellent. The Cather paper was short on concrete examples, as she was well aware.

Her chief gain has been a sense of the reward of patient reading and re-reading. She had dismissed James as a writer who dodged serious issues until she went through *The Ambassadors* a second time.

She also gained insight into the kind of simplification necessary to the social scientist describing trends and forces in a society as compared with the complexities and contradictions in human behavior and feeling as presented by the artist.

William Faulkner (in conference)

I have had three conferences on the work of Faulkner. Miss Rosencrantz has re-read several short stories, "The Bear" and *The Sound and The Fury.* We have discussed other works of Faulkner. She has shown herself to be one of the most perceptive students of his work that I have ever known.

History Essay (outgrowth of *Ideas in America*)

Miss Rosencrantz' work in American history was planned to provide her with a broad background of familiarity with American ideas and institutions. As a member of the class in *Ideas in America,* she studied the eighteenth-century sources of democratic thought and the cluster of European ideas in conflict with the development of democracy. In order to acquire a deeper insight and a firmer grasp, one part of her conference project was devoted to a full analytical comparison between contemporary Danish and American governmental institutions. This obviously involved her in a complicated series of comparisons. She did it very well. I do not think she ever worked harder and I am sure she learned much from this experience.

Although for a time somewhat lost in being plunged into so much American history, Miss Rosencrantz found that her program was soundly planned, and that she is better equipped to teach American literature than she would have been had she concentrated in literature. She believes that it is important for her to understand what the conditions are in the United States which puzzle Europeans. She believes that her field trips, her experiences in the United States, plus the knowledge acquired from her reading, class and conference discussions, have enriched her ability to teach American literature in its appropriate context of culture and tradition.

Discovering a career in social work
through graduate study in theatre

FRANK MARSH, a graduate of Sarah Lawrence in 1949, was one of the young men who had studied at the College in the post-war veterans' program. Frank had become interested in theatre while he was an undergraduate. After leaving college he worked for the most part in some phase of theatre. At the time of his application for the Master's program, Frank was employed part-time as an assistant director of dramatics in a settlement house where he directed plays, organized informal dramatics, and taught acting classes. He wished to return to Sarah Lawrence for graduate work "so that he could improve his teaching methods." His future plan was "to continue working in theatre, probably teaching and acting whenever circumstances permitted."

Frank was admitted to the Graduate Studies Program at the beginning of the second semester, February 1951, and had the following initial program:

1. In theatre, his work consisted of a project in directing and

play production, studying teaching methods in the *Beginning Acting* class and assisting in class teaching and criticism.

2. In psychology, he undertook a conference course on stages of development in children and adolescents. Whenever the material was relevant, he was to attend the class in *Educational Psychology*. Study of children was to be correlated with dramatic techniques in group experiments.

3. In literature, he entered a course in *Shakespeare*.

On March 1, 1951, Frank replied as follows to the question of the Committee on Graduate Studies: Does this program seem adequate to you in terms of your goals?

So far the program is accomplishing two objectives: (1) I am able through my work in *Psychology* better to understand the boys I am teaching in dramatics; (2) I am preparing myself for other related theatre work both with children and adults.

By the end of Frank's first semester several important findings clearly emerged. In evaluating his work his teachers reported:

1. *Theatre*

a. In supervised teaching of students he is doing very good work, understanding their stage of growth, handling them constructively and wisely.

b. In supervising the student directors and in supervising an entire production from casting, putting the play into rehearsal, conferring with design students and faculty on costuming, lighting, and responsibility for the administrative end of the production, Frank demonstrates excellent ability and outstanding work.

2. *Shakespeare*

Although Frank's work is satisfactory and he has written a comprehensive paper covering nine plays, showing that he has acquired background, knows the plots, characters and situation and has a general sense of values in comparing them, he has appeared to have insufficient time, due to the demands of his work in theatre and his part-time work with boys, to develop a working insight into the Shakespearian plays and a method of approach and interpretation which could be applied to other plays or materials.

3. *Psychology*

[In commenting on Frank's work with her, his teacher reviewed the work he had done: reading covering age levels of development, differences in growth rates, some of the effects of these on child relations in a group.] She wrote:

He discussed his observations on his own groups, and since his generalizations sometimes seemed too easy and loose, he took notes on each boy. This led him to revise some of his original generalizations and he began to see the child more sharply both in terms of difference between different groups and among individuals. This material was written up. He utilized both his spontaneous insights and his concepts from reading and translated them into action. He became ingenious and effective in his handling of children much faster than most first year graduate students.

On the other hand, his teacher was impressed with:

his need not only for general concepts in child development but knowledge of dynamics of individual personality including factors involved in problem behavior, psychology of group behavior. Ideally he needed work in the community, the child and the family, adolescence, personality, in order to have a clear picture of the cultural forces affecting children, the emotional factors involved in the child's reaction, the viewing of group experiences and of a group leader for children with different personality needs.

This teacher recommended that Frank continue systematic reading in psychology during the summer, and that he reduce the amount of time working with children at the settlement house. At this point the Committee on Graduate Studies, recognizing Frank's change of interest and need for more concentrated work in psychology, advised for his second semester that "he limit his work at the settlement to two afternoons weekly, limit his work in theatre to one class and devote two-thirds of his program to courses in psychology."

By the beginning of Frank's second semester he had covered the suggested reading while working with children at a summer camp where he was employed as dramatics counsellor. He had many questions from this experience and eagerly discussed course and conference plans with the psychology faculty.

During the second semester, in response to a request from a veterans' hospital, Frank dropped theatre in favor of supervising a project in drama therapy at the College. The plan called for him to organize a group of five students and work, under the direction of the hospital staff, with mentally disturbed patients. The students were to work one period weekly with informal groups on improvisations and short sketches, and to have orientation sessions with the hospital staff, acquainting them with what to expect from the patients. On November 1 Frank's teachers reported:

1. *Theatre*

Frank has been using good judgment in guiding the direction of the work and handling problems which came up with hospital staff and students. His work in general is well-coordinated. He is using his work in psychology to good advantage with his boys' group. His program seems well planned with no sense of rush this term. Very satisfactory work.

2. *Conference Studies in Group Dynamics*

He has a strong inclination to use illustrative material from his group work. In his case this has proved to be of real value and has indicated one of his real assets. He has unusual ability to relate theoretical concepts to his practical activities and vice versa. Another good feature about his work is the sort of questions he raises on the basis of the material. They are rarely concerned with details, although a few attempts to see whether he assimilates facts have been successful. He asks really crucial questions which demand well thought out discussions from me. He follows my comments carefully and introduces observations which push things right along. In this sense our work is real discussion.

His attitude toward the work is exemplary. He is lacking in defensiveness and is quick to take an objective attitude toward situations in which he is involved.

The only fault stems from the pragmatic approach he favors. In reading results of research material he tends to dwell on implications of findings rather than the intentions of the authors.

3. *Conference Studies in Psychology: The Child, the Family and the Community*

Frank has been eager and conscientious. Some of the books he has been reading he had read earlier, but he had never clearly understood or been able to pull together into any kind of framework a concept of personality development.

I think he is beginning to read more carefully, but needs to be limited in amount of reading so that there is sufficient time for him to think about ideas and relate them to his own observation and experiences. There is a naive quality to his thinking at times and he has been able to verbalize his awareness of a wish for simple, direct answers to behavior.

As he has become more aware of the needs of children and the meaning of their behavior he has become more questioning of the program at the settlement where he is working.

I think something very real is happening to Frank in his work, and though he seems only in the beginning of the study of personality development, there has been real change and movement in his thinking from week to week in our conferences.

Both of Frank's psychology teachers were concerned about his lack of supervision at the settlement house. It was possible for them to deepen his understanding of the groups and individuals with whom he was working, but impossible to give him direct supervisory help. Frank's empathy with children, his increasing awareness of problem behavior, his desire to enable children to make positive use of group experience alerted his teachers to his readiness and need for supervised field work. His center of interest had obviously shifted from work in theatre and teaching of dramatics to group work with children or adults, using dramatics as an activity in which he had specialized knowledge and skill. He began to realize that he would need to continue his education in a graduate school of social work. This decision could not have been made prior to his graduate work at Sarah Lawrence, for it was while he was studying for the Master's degree that his ultimate vocational interests became clarified.

Final evaluations by his faculty revealed his continued growth, increased knowledge and developing maturity:

1. *Veterans' Hospital Project*

Frank has completed his assignment at the veterans' hospital in a most satisfactory manner. His supervision of the students' work has been a mature and well-organized experience on a graduate level.

We are very pleased with Frank's development during the past year, both as a student and as a human being.

2. *Conference Studies in Group Dynamics*

Frank is a talented human being, with strong interest and skill in working with children. He has been able to use his course work and include his knowledge of group interaction profitably.

He is an able student who reads and thinks well, particularly in terms of extracting essential points from what he reads.

During the final weeks, I asked him to submit a paper on a topic of his own choosing. He described a group he was working with at the settlement. His first effort was quite thin. It contained interesting ideas which were not developed. Asked to rewrite the paper in a more analytical vein, his second effort was superior to the first, and indicated that he could put his ideas on paper in a well-organized and discursively interesting way. All in all, the work he did was very creditable.

3. *Conference Studies in Psychology: The Child, the Family and the Community*

His interest and response to his reading have been sustained on a high level. He comes to conferences having thought about what he has read, and has a good many questions. He is becoming increasingly clear about the material he does not understand and continues to relate theoretical concepts to his observations of children and adult behavior.

Frank has written a carefully organized, well-written paper on "Ego Development of the Young Child." He pulled together material from his observations, reading and conference discussions into a meaningful whole, revealing good comprehension of basic concepts of child development.

His reading and conference discussions during the past few weeks have been related to the field of social work with particular emphasis on diagnostic and treatment services for children.

Frank's first love, theatre, has given way to an interest in group work with children in which his dramatic skills are only tools for developing a satisfying group experience.

Two years later, Frank writes:

After graduation, I completed my second year at the X Club of New York, doing only dramatics. I then switched over to the Y Settlement as group worker, assisting in all departments. This year, my second, I have been given responsibility for the teen-age boys and the seniors. In the summer, I am the leader of our work camp, a group of thirty-two teen-age boys and girls which is responsible for all maintenance of our camp.

As you can see, my graduate work has resulted directly in all this, and I have been more than content. It's stimulating work, extremely rewarding and more than a substitute for my earlier theatrical ambitions. At the moment, I am considering extended graduate classes next fall.

In sum, I'm doing what I want to, and largely as a result of my decision to enter this field and the good counselling I received.

POSSIBLY the presentation of these seven students provides sufficient details of their learning experiences while studying for the Master's degree to enable the reader to grasp the nature and the extent to which the education of each was tailored to his individual aptitudes, educational background, and goals. Three of these students, who planned to continue their graduate work toward the Ph.D. degree, had a general goal in common but needed different educational experiences. Jan Tesek was planning to teach history,

Karen Rosencrantz and Mrs. Dubois to teach literature. Jan needed research training, and as this progressed it became necessary to change both his original research project and his minor area of study (from philosophy to American literature). Karen Rosencrantz, with extensive preparatory work in American literature, profited from a considerable focus of her work in American history. Mrs. Dubois, who had demonstrated during her undergraduate study her ability to write a critical essay and who had studied literature intensively in specific areas, needed a broader sweep of knowledge of English literature and therefore, for her, an oral examination was more appropriate than a research essay.

The undergraduate concentration of Joan Brent and Ivy Chase in dance and early childhood education, respectively, indicated for them the desirability of a widened scope of learning; consequently two-thirds of their graduate studies were in areas outside their major fields. Perhaps the most significant aspect of Frank Marsh's graduate work was the extent to which his major purpose for graduate study was altered by the impact of his educational experience. Mrs. Winston had the courage to undertake study in a field for which she had had little undergraduate preparation. It would have been far simpler for her to have continued with a major concentration in psychology, but for her as a mature person there was greater satisfaction in tackling the study of history and acquiring a background that would prepare her to teach social studies.

Implicit in our educational planning for all students was the need to clarify for them the philosophy underlying their own programs. In all courses they were encouraged constantly to analyze and evaluate the purposes of their assignments and the teaching methods utilized by their faculty.

In addition to learning about teaching by the ways in which they themselves were taught, these students were prepared for teaching in a variety of situations. Joan Brent was supervised in teaching classes in dance. Karen Rosencrantz attended the undergraduate seminar on educational problems; and she continued her study of European literature primarily to enable her to learn specifically how a course in a foreign literature can be taught. Frank Marsh's teaching experiences included dramatics for children, working with theatre students at the College, and supervising the work of college students in a project away from the campus. Inasmuch as Ivy Chase had been teaching for a number of years prior to her graduate study, there was less emphasis in her program on teaching methods. Mrs. Winston's enrollment in the seminars on *History and Philosophy of Education, Methods of Education,* and *Problems in American Schools* was made necessary by her intention to prepare for both elementary and high school teaching. Finally, all of these students participated in an informal discussion group on educational philosophy conducted bi-weekly by President Taylor as a seminar for graduate students.

The unique value of graduate study in a small college lies in the comprehensive knowledge that teachers have of their students, the flexibility that permits changing programs to meet changing needs, and the opportunity provided for enhancing and deepening students' learning and ways of thinking.

CHAPTER FOUR

Master of Arts Programs in Small Colleges: The Need for a New Concept

JOSEPH CAMPBELL

O N OCTOBER 30, 1953, representatives from a number of colleges in New York, Massachusetts, Connecticut, and Rhode Island assembled at Sarah Lawrence College, on the invitation of the Committee on Graduate Studies, to discuss the problem of the Master's Degree in the small college.[1] Dean Barnaby C. Keeney of Brown University, after briefly stating his views on the present status of the M.A. degree in the United States, presided over the morning session. The question before this session concerned the selection of students. (1) What kind of student (if any) should be advised to work for an M.A. degree? (2) How can a candidate's qualifications be determined? (3) On what are the judgments of a Committee on Graduate Studies to be based: academic records alone, or estimates, also, of the intellectual and personal qualifications of the candidate for his avowed goals?

The second, or afternoon, session of the Conference was devoted to a discussion of the content of the M.A. program and the relation of graduate students on a small campus to the undergraduate college. Professor Charlotte D'Evelyn of Mount Holyoke College presiding, the questions on the agenda were the following: (1) What (if anything) is the essential difference between graduate and undergraduate work? (2) How does a small college determine in what areas to offer its M.A. degree? (3) Should M.A. programs in small colleges be tailor-made within the frame of a fixed standard determined by the faculty, or tailor-made according

---

[1] The participating institutions were: Amherst College, Brown University, Connecticut College, Mount Holyoke College, Trinity College, Vassar College, Wellesley College, Wells College, and Wesleyan University.

to the individual objectives of the students? (4) Does the graduate student take undergraduate courses, and if so, what is his place in these courses and how does he relate to the undergraduates? (5) Are there to be opportunities for prospective teachers to acquire experience in the conduct of classes, aside from the duties generally associated with such tasks as laboratory assistantship and paper correction?

The conference discussions did not adhere strictly to the prepared agenda, but proceeded, in a fruitful and thoughtful manner, to the probing not only of the questions proposed but also of many others. And finally, when, after dinner, President Harold Taylor of Sarah Lawrence College led an informal review of the delegates' general evaluations, the consensus of the conference was that our several small colleges offering the M.A. degree were in a position to make an important contribution to the development of American education, since it had been found that they represented, in their various ways, a body of common principles, values, and aims.

There was, for example, the conviction, which had been expressed in various ways throughout the day, that the strong emphasis on the Ph.D. in large universities and as a general requirement in college teaching had brought the M.A. into disrepute—or at least to a position that made the re-evaluation of its function a necessity. During the morning session the discussion of the present status of the M.A. had centered upon two aspects of the problem: (1) the theoretical and actual relationship of the M.A. degree to the Ph.D., and (2) the differences between the M.A. programs at small liberal arts colleges and those at large universities. It was agreed, as beyond discussion, that any student primarily interested in attaining a Ph.D. degree and in preparing himself either for advanced research or for university teaching should be advised, if well prepared as an undergraduate, to go directly to a large university and commence his graduate work there. For it was clear to all that any young person desiring both to enter upon a professional career and to gain a bit of money and prestige after having done so, must acquire his Ph.D. at the earliest possible instant. Moreover, as Dean Keeney pointed out in his opening remarks, "a man has the best chance of admission to a graduate school giving the doctorate in his field if he has done no graduate work whatsoever; the second best chance if he has a Master's degree from a place that does not give the Ph.D., and a comparatively slight chance if he has an M.A.

from a place giving the Ph.D.—unless there are good reasons that he should change—assuming equal quality." "All of us," the Dean added, "who are concerned with graduate work feel badly about this, and most of us who are concerned with undergraduate instruction rather deplore the tendency in recent years virtually to require a doctorate as a license for teaching.

"I see no very good reason," he then stated—and these words sounded the keynote of the conference—"why the Master's degree cannot be rehabilitated, but I doubt very much that it will be in institutions that give the doctorate. It is much more likely that it will be restored to respectability in colleges which do not give the doctorate except occasionally."

Good reasons for such a hope were supplied by most of the delegates during the course of the conference; for it was clear to all—as it has been to us in our work with graduate students at Sarah Lawrence College—that for certain types of students there is a distinct advantage to be derived from a year on a small college campus, even if the intention is to go forward to a Ph.D. Of these types there is, in the first place, the so-called "late bloomer": the student who, in the course of his undergraduate career, came late to the realization that he would be interested in graduate work and who, consequently, is insufficiently grounded in the sort of general knowledge of his field that is simply taken for granted in the normal graduate school. For such a student, the individually adjustable and flexible program that a small college can offer has a distinct advantage, since it can supply in a concentrated way precisely the information and experience in which he is deficient, while taking as much advantage as possible of whatever broader knowledge or interests he may possess as a consequence of earlier studies outside of the range of his newly found field of specialization. We have had examples of this type of student in our Sarah Lawrence program (for example, Mrs. Dubois, discussed in the preceding chapter), and from the reports that we have received from some of these students in the course of their work for their Ph.D. degrees, it is safe to say that the kind of particular attention they received on our small campus prepared them excellently for the work in the more highly specialized courses of the large universities.

One might add, as a sub-class to this type of the "late bloomer," the slightly older young man or woman who, having left the academic world for a time, now desires to return and take a Ph.D.

Many members of the conference appeared to agree, furthermore, that a student who intended to go on to a Ph.D. but was unclear as to his specific interests, might benefit from a year of work toward an M.A. on a smaller campus where, with special attention, he might gain clarity as to his goals. From our experience at Sarah Lawrence College, however, it would appear that great caution should be exercised in dealing with candidates in this category of the "unclear goal." It is curious, but candidates who are unclear in their goals, yet full of premonitions of the possibilities of clarification, frequently present very cogent and charming pictures of themselves on their admissions forms and in their preliminary interviews; often, furthermore, flattering, in a very subtle, half-unconscious way, the pedagogical susceptibilities of their interviewers, who may tend to project into the fairly blank field of the searching student's active mind all of their high hopes for their own capacities as teachers. This leads to hopeful plans and disgraceful miscarriages. Practically all of our failures have been with students of this type.

The principal interest of the colleges represented at the conference was not, however, in the M.A. degree as a prelude to the Ph.D., but in the M.A. as a goal in itself; either for students wishing to prepare and qualify for teaching, or for those wishing to round out and intensify their understanding of some chosen field, either (a) preliminary to work in some profession, for example, journalism or research, or (b) simply for personal reorientation and self-discovery. The type (b) student of course is hardly different from the pre-Ph.D. candidate of "unclear goal," discussed above. Yet one of the institutions represented at our conference reported a considerable program for candidates of this category. A number of speakers, furthermore, suggested that they saw no inherent contradiction in planning for all three types of program, since they had values in common.

In general, it was felt that it was in the area of graduate education for teachers that the smaller colleges could make their important contribution. As Dean Keeney phrased the case in his opening remarks: "Colleges of the sort represented here can make an enormous contribution to secondary education by working out a Master's degree in teaching that has some meaning. . . . There have been many complaints about the preparation of college teachers also," he continued. "Many Ph.D. candidates have a lack of interest and experience in teaching, and an insufficient acquaintance with education. Even industrialists complain that the students in chemistry are over-specialized." Exquisite specialization, a primary interest in research, and an almost absolute indifference to the personal development of the student, may have a place in certain departments of our educational system, but certainly not in those devoted to the fostering of emotional maturity and the humane illumination of the mind. In such fields as law, theology, physical science, archaeology, mathematics, and philology, where technical skills, large bodies of fixed material, and inherited traditions of interpretation have to be mastered, the youth who has passed an honest examination can be presumed to be a less precarious employment risk than the one who has failed. However, in the fields of creative literature, music, and the arts—perhaps also (ironically) in philosophy itself—a degree of Doctor of Philosophy may be a sign of trained incapacity. If one takes seriously the qualifications of a teacher cited in Chapter One above, from the words of Dean Harry J. Carman of Columbia University and Professor Lloyd S. Woodburne of the University of Michigan, one cannot but be amazed that in the majority of our universities the *sine qua non* for teaching is not any one or two of the attributes there so nobly announced, but the Ph.D.

The delegates to the Sarah Lawrence Conference on Graduate Study in the Small College not only agreed that the preparation of teachers was the matter of their chief concern, but also found that they had a fairly clear notion of what the training programs should be. For the most part, their immediate focus was rather on secondary school than on college teaching. Some of the institutions represented already had ambitious programs under way in this field; most of the others were either training a small number of prospective teachers or making plans for the initiation of such training. It was pointed out that many secondary school systems now are requiring an M.A. degree, but it was felt that in too many instances our M.A. degree programs in education concentrate rather on courses in education than on a training in, and study of, the modern approaches to the subject matters to be taught. It was observed repeatedly by the members of the Sarah Lawrence Conference that our group of small colleges with M.A. programs can make a valuable contribution to the cause of education in the United States if they will attempt to give a truly cultural value and reality to this at-present insignificant degree.

The large universities are not in a position to effect the reform, since their graduate schools are predominantly and incorrigibly research-minded. The small colleges, on the other hand, while rendering sufficient training in techniques and current rules of research to enable their future teachers to know the relationship of new discoveries in their various fields to the fundamental values, categories, and disciplines of their interest, are disposed to concentrate rather on the general relationship of the materials of scholarship to the normal ends of a liberal arts education—the development, that is to say, of mature, well-rounded individuals, specialized in a manner appropriate to their talents, inspired in their learning by an idea of humane culture, and aware of their responsibilities in a democratic society.

The small colleges, furthermore, besides giving an excellent general training in their subjects, can see to it that their candidates preparing to teach have some actual experience in teaching and in adjusting their evaluations not only to the demands of their personal lives and ideals but also to the problems and limitations of their future pupils. For the potential teacher, as well as learning how to study, must also learn to teach. He must select and arrange the materials of his field with a view, not only to a systematic, but also to a pedagogical continuity; and he must train himself to present his learning lucidly, dispassionately, and in such a manner as to evoke some significant participation from his class. His intellectual decorum and personal character must be such that his students will have some tangible evidence of the pertinence of his subject to human life. On the small college campus the aspirant to the teaching career can be watched closely not only in his learning but also in his teaching performance, and those who give evidence of inherent personal, intellectual, or emotional difficulties as a teacher, can be advised to go on to specialized research and the Ph.D.

It was reported by a number of the delegates to the conference that their respective colleges had found it possible to arrange for teaching opportunities with the local school systems; and at Sarah Lawrence also we have had this experience. At one of the colleges the program for the M.A. degree requires two years of work, the

100

time being divided between study and a considerable schedule of practice teaching. Moreover, for those wishing to teach in college, it was generally felt that there should be devised some form of internship, comparable, perhaps, to those now being sponsored by the Carnegie Corporation and the Ford Foundation for candidates for the Ph.D. It was suggested, for example, that where graduate students participate in undergraduate classes, it might be arranged for them to take over, in some measure, the conduct of the class.

In this connection there was considerable discussion, also, of the role of the laboratory assistantship. Whereas, on the one hand, the danger of the practice being converted into a routine form of cheap labor was indicated, it was also maintained that important educational experiences were to be derived from such work. There was a general feeling that, although on a large campus the duties of a laboratory assistant might well—and actually often do—degenerate into a schedule of mechanical or even menial routines, in the more intimate environment of the small colleges, candidates benefit from the guidance of their experienced instructors and are introduced by them, through the medium of their laboratory duties, to many of the problems that they will face later in their teaching.

There was a lively discussion of the varieties of instruction that might be offered by the smaller colleges to their candidates for the M.A. degree. Since, in the small college, the number of graduate students working in a given field at any given time is always small, it has not been found practical to organize specific graduate courses of instruction. As at Sarah Lawrence, so elsewhere, some sort of individual tutorial work has been worked out as the most effective method of procedure. Indeed, even in those colleges where graduate courses are listed in the catalogues, they are given usually only in alternate years, and then of course to not more than two or three students at a time. Moreover, in the off years they may be offered to a single student if appropriate.

A second form of graduate instruction that appeared to be common on the small college campuses is the seminar offered jointly to M.A. candidates and advanced majors or honors students in the undergraduate program. A third is the advanced undergraduate course. And a fourth—which evoked considerable discussion—is the elementary course for the M.A. candidate requiring a new skill; for example, mathematics or a language. Certain institutions considered this to be a legitimate part of a graduate program; others maintained that such work should be carried on a non-credit basis.

A great deal of consideration was given to the problem of the relation of undergraduate goals in education to graduate instruction. The consensus seemed to be that, in addition to its being a necessity, it was academically both legitimate and desirable for M.A. candidates to work in courses and seminars with advanced undergraduates. It was urged, for example, that the goals of intellectual maturity and of competence in any given subjects are finally the same for the two groups, and that in classes where both graduates and undergraduates are represented, all that need be demanded additionally of the M.A. candidate is an advanced and comparatively secure performance level. There is a value, moreover, to an undergraduate class, in the stimulus of the presence of a graduate student and, reciprocally, there is a value to the M.A. candidate in the opportunity to learn something of the methods and problems of college teaching through close observation.

Perhaps the crucial problem in the organization and development of a graduate program on a small campus is that of the selection of the candidates. There was comparatively little discussion of this important matter at our October conference, but in our experience in our own graduate program at Sarah Lawrence College we have found that as our techniques of selection have improved, the performance level of our candidates has risen and the proportion of withdrawals has been appreciably reduced.

The first thing we learned, as already noted, is that the applicants for admission to a graduate school cannot be treated as adults knowing what they want and how to get it. Neither can they be judged as disembodied intellects, whose academic work alone is to be our concern. A number large enough to be important are profoundly confused young people, hoping to postpone certain life decisions by remaining in the incubator, and all have emotional problems which, on occasion, may rise to threaten or subvert the projects of the mind. In the first year of our Program, 1950-1951, we did not know what *kinds* of information we should have from our students before considering them; we did not confront them with the right questions in our admissions form; and consequently of the eight admitted, five were ill-qualified, and of these, four soon left the campus (three withdrew, one transferred). We have made

102

few such mistakes since. Both the questions we now ask on our admissions form and the techniques we employ in our interviews have enabled us to avoid undue risks in selection. We have learned also to be chary of candidates who cannot formulate good clear working purposes for their interest in the degree. We do best, we have found, with students whose specific purposes we know, whose previous education can be properly supplemented on our own campus through courses or conferences leading in the directions in which they ought to go, and for whom every step of the planning has some bearing on their needs and desires. Occasionally this means that during the course of the year it will be found that the goal with which the student came was inappropriate (as, for example, in the case of Frank Marsh, summarized in Chapter Three), when it will be necessary for us to assist the candidate toward formulating new goals. But our troubles of this kind have been remarkably few, and fortunately the intimate nature of our tutorial teaching has made it possible for us to guide the two most notable cases of this kind to fresh discoveries that were at once appropriate and significant.

We have learned, furthermore, to limit our expectations: not to attempt to help our graduate students make up for all the deficiencies of their former lives and education; not to set up impressive criteria that cannot be met; but rather to be quite specific about what each student is to accomplish with each teacher.

In the cases of foreign students the risks of admission are much more difficult to measure, however; and it cannot be said, either on the basis of our own experience or on that of the findings of our October conference, that a solution or satisfactory approach to this problem has been found. For it is extremely difficult to determine at what level the applicant from abroad should be advised to work; as a candidate for the A.B., for the M.A., or as a special student. Moreover, because of language or cultural difficulties, such students cannot always complete the work for the M.A. in the single year available to them for study in the United States. One institution reported giving to such students a certificate to the effect that they had completed a year of work in a particular field, and it was agreed that such certificates might be useful. They cannot compensate, however, for the distress and disappointment that will be general until a greater experience of trans-oceanic exchanges has made it possible for our admissions committees to estimate the

103

potentialities of the products of the various foreign systems of education.

But no less important—finally—than the college's judgment of the applicant for admission is the college's judgment and evaluation of its own capacity to teach. At Sarah Lawrence, during the second year of our Graduate Program (1951-1952), the faculty Committee on Graduate Studies instituted a program of discussion and observation throughout the whole College to determine what areas of the College curriculum were best suited for work on the graduate level. In 1950-1951 one student specialized in literature, two in social science and history, three in psychology and child study, one in dance, and one in art. In 1951-1952 one was specializing in social science and history, one in psychology and child study, one in the dance, and two in art. In 1952-1953 three specialized in literature, two in literature and history, one in psychology and child study, and four in the dance. In 1953-1954 one specialized in history, one in history and literature, one in philosophy, one in psychology, one in art, and three in dance. To date, none has specialized in physical science, in biology, or in music.

Through its series of meetings with the several faculties of the College in 1951-1952, the Committee sought to institute a general consideration of the problems of graduate teaching, but also, and more particularly, to conduct precise discussions of the requirements, standards, and facilities of the various college departments. And it was found that, of the areas of study in which graduate work had not yet been pursued at Sarah Lawrence College, music was one in which we were particularly well prepared. In physics, on the other hand, the College was not equipped for graduate study, since we have neither the library nor the laboratories for advanced research. And in the biological sciences our chief contribution would probably be in the training of students who expected to teach biology in the secondary schools. In our undergraduate program we have successfully experimented in the teaching of human biology to beginning students, and this instruction can be extended to the graduate program. For the candidate for an M.A. degree who comes to us with a conventional major in the biological sciences, we could readily plan a program that would considerably enlarge her scope and give her new ways of planning the teaching of biology for young students.

In languages and philology, the facilities of the College were

104

found to be more limited, particularly the library facilities. In literature, modern history, social science, painting, and the performing arts, on the other hand, we have achieved very good results. Indeed, we believe that it is in these latter departments that our main contribution can be made. In psychology the College is best equipped for specialized work in child study.

Comparably, the delegates from the other small colleges who attended our October conference were able to report various fields in which they had found themselves to be particularly competent. Professor Plough of Amherst, for example, named biology as the subject in which Amherst had awarded the largest number of M.A. degrees, and Professor Applezweig of Connecticut College cited chemistry, botany, and zoology. From the discussion it appeared that if a proper system of intercollegiate communication could be established and maintained, the smaller colleges offering M.A. programs would be able to function as a coordinated single force in the field of American education, representing, not a reaction against, or criticism of, the comparatively impersonal and standardized approach of the universities, but an additional, or rather alternative, approach to graduate teaching, appropriate to certain types of students that are not well served—indeed, whose intellectual careers and development are occasionally wrecked—by the instruction commonly offered on the larger campus.

It became very clear, during the course of our conference, that Sarah Lawrence College is not alone in its effort to explore and establish the possibilities of an approach to teaching on the graduate level that will foster a development of the student—and particularly of the potential teacher—more closely in accord with the commonly expressed and generally accepted ideals of a liberal arts education than is possible in the specialized graduate schools of our major American universities. There are differences of emphasis on the smaller campuses, not only in fields of study offered but also in educational ideals and standards. For example, there was considerable discussion at the conference of the extent to which possible standard requirements in a given area of study should be allowed to predetermine the pattern of an M.A. program. At one extreme was the statement of Professor Charlotte D'Evelyn of Mount Holyoke College that although the college has a responsibility to the individual student, it has also a responsibility to the subject. "There is a place where the subject is more important than the individual student," she declared. "No one college can set up its own standards; for there is a community of knowledge, of information, and of standards that has to be recognized if a college is going to give the accepted degree." The most radical statement in opposition to this stand was that of President Harold Taylor of Sarah Lawrence, who suggested that all of us interested in education should feel free to question the content of subject matter regarded as traditional in our field. "A philosophy that emphasizes quality in learning," he believed, "and that looks at material with a query as to whether it can move one in new and significant directions is quite acceptable—and particularly in relation to work for the M.A." He suggested that in the smaller colleges, where the student-teacher relationship is of a close and comparatively intimate nature, "we might play with this new concept in education instead of simply striving to meet certain set requirements." Professor Herdman of Trinity College then observed that this, actually, was not a new concept in education at all. "While it may be new on the graduate level," he said, "we have quite a historical precedent for such an attitude in the education of young children."

And here, it might be observed, is the main point of the whole program. Where the growth and blossoming of a personality is an aim in education, the presentation of subject matter is to be governed by the educator's estimate of the pupil's need, capacity, and direction of interest. The so-called objective standards of the subject can be stressed only to a certain point—the point where they begin to deaden what may be termed the student's experience of the life of his subject. Ultimately, of course, the so-called objective standards are themselves not objective absolutely, but only in relation to a certain accepted point of view with respect to the subject matter in question. What an art historian might regard as an objective standard for the understanding and interpretation of art, for example, a practicing artist might regard as a pitiful joke. Likewise, the poet's notion of what a student of literature should learn will not closely correspond to that of the philologist. Standards, no matter how sound they may seem to be to the people who like them, have to be understood as functions of a certain way of life; and if the life that they are to further is killed in the course of meeting their demands, the primary function of the act of education is defeated. The paramount aim of the educational ideal of Sarah Lawrence College, and of the majority of the institutions represented at our Conference on Graduate Study in the Small College, might be said to be to carry the *vital* principle in education as far up the scale as it can be made to go: beginning at the level of the nursery school, and continuing on up through college even into the desert land of Carlyle's "dry as dust." The problem was succinctly summarized by Professor Plough of Amherst when he said that every institution has to decide what its M.A. shall be, "in terms of greater maturity; in the understanding of how true knowledge is accumulated. If you set up standards of this kind," he said, "then you can neglect, to some extent, the other things."

Under the sign of this governing principle it will be obvious that the critical question is not whether objective standards are to be met or scheduled quantities of material conveyed into the student's head, but rather, in each particular case, what quantity and aspect of the traditional material the student is ready to receive. Where a perfect accord is found and complete readiness, the full load of the discipline, as understood by the teacher, can be delivered without fear of death; but where learning difficulties or resistances appear, the teacher must be ready to concede that his student may be struggling for a vital insight or system of values not quite in accord with those cherished by himself and his distinguished colleagues in the teaching profession. In such an instance the teacher must become an educator indeed: one who seeks to "bring out" the latent potentialities of the student, to find for these a field in which to develop, and then to assist the student toward a profitable employment of his particular talents within the frame of our democratic society. Between those delegates to the conference who favored standardized requirements and those who were concerned, rather, with building a program around individual needs, there was a considerable area of agreement, inasmuch as it was generally conceded that for any teaching candidate, a broad minimal knowledge of the field in question was essential. But it was conceded also that there are in this country a great number of graduate students aspiring to teaching posts who might better be aspiring to something else; and that on the small campus the aberrant potentialities of these confused young people can be recognized, and their efforts to "find themselves" significantly aided. Furthermore, the propriety of requiring teaching candidates to spend the critical years of their learning career in studies designed to fit them not for teaching but for specialized research was

107

unanimously questioned—and again, the serviceability of the small campus as a field where neglected potentialities might be recognized was unanimously conceded: the neglected potentialities to be rescued, in this case, not of confused young people, but of a confused educational system.

Simultaneously, the potentialities of our students and those of our humane intellectual inheritance can be explored—indeed, are *being explored*—on the smaller campuses of this country. At Sarah Lawrence College we have long been involved in this important movement, and we are committed to continue to explore, to apply our findings to new ranges of education, and to create teachers competent to perpetuate and disseminate our patterns of teaching and educational research. From the point of view of the graduate students who have worked with us, it is clear that, without exception, those who continued with us and received their M.A. degrees gained something that could not have been supplied by the graduate school of any large university—namely, close attention from the faculty of their individual requirements, talents, and deficiencies, and a chance to "find themselves" in their chosen fields of study. The flexibility of the student's program gives us an opportunity to meet whatever needs may appear as the originally-made plans develop. In several cases the crisis of self-discovery was radical and remarkably clear. And, simultaneously, from the point of view of the College, the chief value of our Graduate Studies Program is that it is enabling us to advance our experiment in individual education from the undergraduate to the graduate level, while training teachers to carry the philosophy and practices to other schools and colleges. We have also found, furthermore, that whereas the concept of the M.A. degree in this country is confused, our own experience suggests a possible basis for new definitions and functional standards. And, finally, we have discovered, through the Conference, that there is support for our position in the work being done on other campuses, to such an extent that it would require only a coordinating mechanism and effort to convert the various separate experiments into a single dynamic contribution to the cause of American education.

One great obstacle and threat to the whole experiment must be noted, however, before this summation of our procedure and findings can be brought to a close; namely, the difficulty of attracting competent candidates, and particularly those who might become good teachers. For college graduates at the tops of their classes are being lured increasingly from the fields of learning to positions in business and industry, for which the A.B. is a sufficient preparation, at beginning salaries far higher than the initial salaries in teaching for which, furthermore, expensive additional training is required. Young men and women genuinely interested in teaching as a profession are being discouraged by this financial factor and further discouraged by the things they hear and read about the conditions prevalent in many of our secondary schools. If their desire to teach is strong, they usually aim at nursery and elementary, or at college teaching. This situation cannot be remedied immediately. No doubt, the general concern about the need for improving our secondary education will eliminate a number of the adverse factors, but the process will be slow—and rendered the slower by a growing dearth of adequate teachers.

It is necessary, in the meantime, for graduate schools to consider seriously all those applicants who seem to have even a moderate chance of success. On the larger campuses, multitudes of mediocre people are accepted, and multitudes, after a period of study, simply dissolve away. This is a pattern of procedure excessively wasteful of the country's mentality and youth. In our own screening operations we collect, through careful inquiry, preliminary information from the individuals who indicate an interest in our program, and the Committee then attempts to decide which are the appropriate candidates, before allowing them to make their formal application. Those who seem to be good candidates, but with interests that might better be served at some other college or at a university, are advised to explore the other educational possibilities before deciding to apply at Sarah Lawrence College. And if, on the other hand, the inquirer seems not to be qualified or ready for graduate work, appropriate counsel has been offered.

The number of students that we have considered and the number that we have accepted is still too small for any significant analysis to be compiled. From our general observation of the field, however, and from our experience in the education of those students who have come to us, the Committee holds the belief that there are in this country many sound candidates for the M.A. degree who require individualized teaching in a small college, and that in default of such teaching our profession is losing perhaps some of the best and most promising of its rare candidates every year. The reports from the participants in our October conference have confirmed our belief. A co-ordinated system for directing such students might well be organized on a regional basis through an exchange of information such as occurred at our conference. If the colleges were more adequately prepared financially to meet not only the attraction of the fellowships and scholarships being offered today so liberally by the graduate schools of the larger universities, but also the challenge of industry and business, both our students and our colleges could make their choices on a sound educational basis.

In brief, then, there is a need in the American educational field today for both financial and intellectual support in the graduate field for the values of humanistic, as distinguished from research, scholarship; there is a need for student-oriented programs; and there is a need felt by many students for close supervision from teachers interested not only in their own professional knowledge and techniques, but also in the application of their wisdom to alien academic, or even non-academic, fields of experience and realization. The large campus is ill-adapted to facilitate the adjustments necessary for such education; the small campus, on the other hand, has already demonstrated its usefulness for this purpose. The ideals of the program in operation at Sarah Lawrence College are in essence identical with those that have inspired the teaching in our institution since its founding, namely those concerned with the development of intelligent, mature individuals—in this special work, however, directed primarily to the career of teaching.

Appendixes

The Sarah Lawrence Undergraduate Program

IN A BOOK of this scope on graduate studies, a full and adequate description of the philosophy and methods of undergraduate education at Sarah Lawrence is precluded. Apart from the brief description on page *xviii* of President Taylor's Introduction, and scattered explanations in the course of the succeeding chapters, some familiarity on the part of readers with the educational values and procedures of Sarah Lawrence College is necessarily assumed. For the reader who is totally unfamiliar, or who wishes to extend his information further, the following list of publications concerning the work of the College is provided.

A New Design for Women's Education, Constance Warren. Frederick A. Stokes Company, 1940.

Literature for Individual Education, Esther Raushenbush. Columbia University Press. Sarah Lawrence College Publications, No. 1, 1942.

Psychology for Individual Education, Lois B. Murphy, Eugene Lerner, Jane Judge, Madeleine Grant. Edited by Esther Raushenbush. Columbia University Press. Sarah Lawrence College Publications, No. 2, 1942.

Teaching the Individual, Ruth Munroe. Columbia University Press. Sarah Lawrence College Publications, No. 3, 1942.

Emotional Factors in Learning, Lois B. Murphy and Henry Ladd. Columbia University Press. Sarah Lawrence College Publications, No. 4, 1944.

Field Work in College Education, Helen Merrell Lynd. Columbia University Press. Sarah Lawrence College Publications, No. 5, 1945.

Essays in Teaching, thirteen essays by members of the Sarah Lawrence faculty. Edited by Harold Taylor. Harper Bros., 1950.

On Education and Freedom, Harold Taylor. Abelard-Schuman, 1954.

Note on Finances

D URING the first four years of graduate study at Sarah Lawrence, on which this book is based, the College was fortunate in having the grant of $50,000 from the Carnegie Corporation to enable it to establish the program. Without this grant the program could not have materialized.

How this money was used may be of some general interest. The grant was for four years, in which $10,000 was to be spent annually, and the remaining $10,000 to be a fund for publications and other such adjunct activities. As stated in Chapter One, the normal graduate tuition of $500 set in 1950 could not possibly cover the cost of a student's education. Certainly it did not compare with the Sarah Lawrence undergraduate day student tuition charge of $1,000, and this was estimated by the Comptroller's Office of the College to be roughly $500 below actual cost. The college was, then, in fact granting a scholarship of $1,000 to every graduate student who paid the full tuition.

Since there was no way to arrive at precise figures as to the share of the various costs of the College that might be allocated to the Graduate Studies Program, some arbitrary budgetary allotments were set up, including only those charges in which it was possible to make some estimate of actual cost, and simply excluding all other costs. For example, the Graduate Studies Program was not charged any share of the plant and housekeeping expenses of the College. On the other hand, a major part of the $10,000 that was to be spent annually was allocated to the faculty-salary budget—namely $8,000. It was considered necessary not to make any special appointments of faculty to teach graduate students, but to enlarge the available faculty teaching-time through this sum in order to absorb, in part, the additional burden of the teaching of graduate students.

115

Another item of $1,500 was assigned to the nursery school to help cover the additional expense due to the practice teaching and observation of graduate students. An additional $500 was given to the library budget for the purchase of books; $2,000 was allocated for secretarial and administrative costs; $500 for supplies and expense, and $1,500 for scholarships. That total of $14,000 was covered by the $10,000 from the Carnegie Corporation grant, plus roughly $4,000 income from tuition of our usual eight graduate students at $500 each. In every other respect the College carried the program financially, and in effect granted it an endowment out of undergraduate tuition income. It should also be stated, perhaps, that the program was not in any sense conducted lavishly, and that, in fact, such important activities as adequate publicity and recruiting of students had to be passed-by for financial reasons.

Income:	from Grant	$10,000	
	Tuition	4,000	*varied*
		$14,000	
Expenses:	Faculty Salaries	$8,000	
	Nursery School	1,500	
	Books	500	
	Scholarships	1,500	*varied*
	Secretarial Services	2,000	
	Supplies and Expense	500	*varied*
		$14,000	

Any portion of funds as budgeted that were not used up were placed in a reserve, and in the spring of 1954 the Carnegie Corporation also permitted the supplies and expense item to be charged to the fund for publication. This provided a total of $6,900 which was applied to the costs of the Graduate Studies Program during 1954-55. The remainder of the costs, less tuition, was carried by the undergraduate budget and by the faculty who undertook graduate instruction in addition to their regular duties. During 1955-56, the program has had to be carried entirely by the College and the faculty. For this year the tuition was raised to $700 and no scholarships were granted. It was the decision of the faculty and the Board

116

of Trustees of the College that the program should be continued, temporarily at least, on this basis until some further source of funds could be secured. Whether the College will be able to support this program it has found so valuable without new financial resources is at present an open question.

Participants in the Conference
on Graduate Study in the Small College

October 30, 1953

Mortimer Applezweig, *Psychology, Connecticut College*
Ruth Conklin, *Physiology, Vassar College*
Marjorie Crawford, *Chemistry, Vassar College*
Charlotte D'Evelyn, *English, Mount Holyoke College*
Ross A. Gortner, Jr., *Biochemistry, Wesleyan University*
Donald L. Herdman, *Education, Trinity College*
Adolf Katzenellenbogen, *Committee on Fellowships and Graduate Study, Vassar College*
Barnaby C. Keeney, *Dean of the College,* Brown University*
L. J. Long, *President of Wells College*
Adolph F. Pauli, *Committee on Graduate Instruction, Wesleyan University*
Harold Plough, *Biology, Amherst College*
C. Scott Porter, *Dean of Amherst College*
Dorothy Robathan, *Committee on Graduate Instruction, Wellesley College*
Marion Tait, *Dean of Vassar College*
D. G. Brinton Thompson, *History and Political Science, Trinity College*
Robert M. Vogel, *English, Trinity College*

*Now President

Participants in Conference

Harold Taylor, *President*
Esther Raushenbush, *Dean of the College*

Elizabeth Beeman, *Science*	Helen McMaster, *Literature*
Adda Bozeman, *Social Science*	Madalyn O'Shea, *Theatre Arts*
Adele Brebner, *Literature*	Kurt Roesch, *Art*
Joseph Campbell, *Literature*	Bessie Schonberg, *Dance*
George Goethals, *Psychology*	Andre Singer, *Music*
Madeleine Grant, *Science*	Marc Slonim, *Literature*
Edmund Haines, *Music*	Edward Solomon, *Social Science*
Maurice Irvine, *Literature*	Bernard Steinzor, *Psychology*
Jane G. Judge, *Psychology*	Harold Wiener, *Literature*

Bert James Loewenberg, *Social Science*

A Graduate Program in an Undergraduate College

has been printed directly from type by letterpress. It has been composed in Linotype *Caledonia,* a type designed for machine composition by W. A. Dwiggins. Though completely contemporary, Caledonia was influenced by several Scotch models, and owes an acknowledged debt to the type originally cut by William Martin, in the late eighteenth century, for William Bulmer. Another current version of Martin's letter, and one which attempts to follow the original much more closely, is *Bulmer,* the type appearing in the chapter titles and other display lines in this book.

WESLEYAN UNIVERSITY PRESS